A Year of Highland Archaeology

A Collection of the Projects and Activities of the North of Scotland Archaeological Society

Editorial team:
**Jonie Guest, Meryl Marshall,
James McComas, Roland Spencer-Jones**

James McComas → 29.9.19

Bassman Books

Published by Bassman Books, Burnside Cottage, Newhall, Balblair, Dingwall, IV7 8LT

First published in 2019

A catalogue record for this book is available from the British Library

ISBN 978-0-9956440-3-8

Printed by Big Sky, The Press Building, 305 The Park, Findhorn, Forres, IV36 3TE

Layout and design by Russell Turner www.russellturner.org Set in Palatino 10.5/13pt

NOSAS became a charity in 2014, registered no. SCO44585 with the Scottish Charity Regulator

Cover photo: Tarradale Through Time excavation at Mesolithic shell midden site, October 2017.

MIX
Paper from
responsible sources

FSC
www.fsc.org
FSC® C020891

Contents

Foreword

In 2018 NOSAS celebrated 20 successful years of its existence, during which it has developed into a thriving and dynamic group willing and eager to investigate new fields of archaeology and take on new challenges. Over the years we have undertaken many projects, gaining in knowledge, experience and understanding. In the recent past we have embraced new ways to use digital technology in the study of archaeology in the North of Scotland.

This publication describes some of the archaeological projects and activities undertaken over recent years. Some have been carried out using long established methods, such as field walking and plane-tabling. Others have used more digital techniques, such as photogrammetry and drones. All, however, are enjoyed by an enthusiastic band of local amateur archaeologists.

These ten articles provide a varied, interesting, even experimental, programme of our undertakings. It seemed totally fitting that we should collect them into a publication. There was no shortage of members coming forward with contributions for it. Many thanks to you all; and many thanks to all those who have helped and encouraged NOSAS over the years. Enjoy!

Jonie, Meryl, James & Roland – the editorial team

1: NOSAS – The Early Years

by Meryl Marshall

A yearbook produced in the 20th year of our Society cannot pass without reflection on some of the activities of the group, its development and its achievements over the 20 years. Since 1998 NOSAS has grown from a small inexperienced group of 11 founding members to a thriving active group of over 120 members today. There have been many interesting and memorable experiences along the way. It is proposed here to focus on the earlier years, but also to include something of the journey to more recent times.

In 1998 an assorted group of people gathered together at the Blacksmiths Inn, Culloden Moor. They included an ex-pilot, several teachers, some engineers, a solicitor and an ex-police inspector; eleven people all sharing a keen interest in archaeology. *But who were they and how did they come to be there?* Three years earlier, in the autumn of 1995, 44 people had met in the bar of the Millburn Hotel, Inverness (now the Premier Inn). They were brought together by an advert in the Inverness Courier which proposed a course in Scottish Field Archaeology. The course was to be run as face to face evening lectures over a three year period and would lead to a Certificate in Scottish Field Archaeology. It would be funded jointly by Highland Council, the Scottish Vernacular Buildings Trust and the University of Aberdeen Centre for Continuing Education. John Wood, head archaeologist for Highland Council at the time, was to take a lead role. There was a lot of enthusiasm amongst the group but also some apprehension – how would they cope with the rigours of academia, sitting exams and the like?

Twenty-four people turned up for the first lecture at Culloden Academy. The principal tutors were John Wood and Dorothy Lowe. Later Robin Hanley, Alison Fox and others would have input. For

Fig. 1: The eleven completers of the Aberdeen Course who founded NOSAS in 1998

Fig. 2: The Easter Raitts excavation 1996-1999

Fig. 3: Training at Banchor township

them it was perhaps a challenge dealing with a group of mature opinionated folk who would be forever asking questions. In addition to the lectures there were several field outings, to sites such as the Pictish Cemetery at Whitebridge and Kinloss Abbey. This latter site in particular made quite an impression. It was one of the first monasteries to be established in the Highlands, founded in 1141 by David I. Yet it was in a desperate state, having been robbed of much of its stonework and now extremely neglected and overgrown. It was ideal for the "SWOT analysis" that was required and which was the purpose of the visit. Since then it is pleasing to note that the site has received much more attention. The course included practical sessions such as geophysics at Cromarty House, and a compulsory annual week of excavation based on the township of Easter Raitts in Badenoch. This township would later be re-constructed at the Highland Folk Museum, Newtonmore by the Scottish Vernacular Buildings Trust.

After three years, 11 "completers" received their awards. However, they had lots of ideas for further practical projects and were keen to continue their interest. So they formed the North of Scotland Archaeological Society, holding their inaugural meeting at the Blacksmiths Inn in the Autumn of 1998. Put simply, the objective of the Society was "to further the study of archaeology in the North of Scotland and to promote that interest to a wider audience".

Over the next few years the group gradually gained in confidence, helped and encouraged by professionals from such organisations as the Highland Council HER team, the Royal Commission for Historic and Ancient Monuments (RCAHMS – now part of HES), and Scotland's Coastal Archaeology and the Problem of Erosion (SCAPE) project. The group members were aware that they needed to maintain the high standards that had been drilled into them on the course. Several weekend field courses in interpretation, recording and surveying, run by the RCAHMS and held at Ben Lawers and in Glen Banchor, Newtonmore, were particularly helpful; these were replaced by the Scotland Rural Past team in 2006. Training has always been, and still is, an important part of the NOSAS programme. Several members continued to do modules through the University of Aberdeen and some have even completed degrees.

Twenty years ago digital cameras did not exist and photography

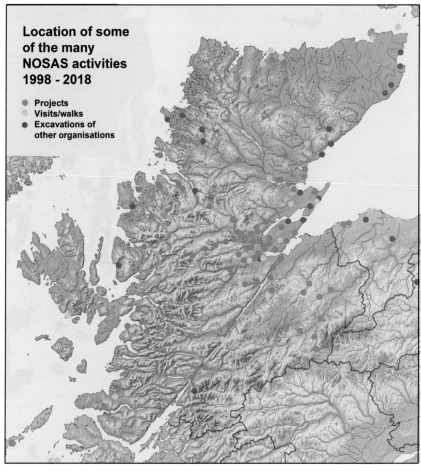

Location of some of the many NOSAS activities 1998 - 2018

- Projects
- Visits/walks
- Excavations of other organisations

Fig. 4: Locations of NOSAS activities 1998-2018

Fig. 5: Torrisdale broch near Bettyhill

was much less convenient. GPS units were less accurate and there was no such thing as the internet, email or smart phones. Newsletters, mostly sent out by post, were important for keeping the group together. The first one in June 1999 flagged up a bus trip to the National Museum of Scotland in Edinburgh, the second one welcomed new members John Wombell, Paul Humphreys, Marion Ruscoe and Anne Wakeling - all still familiar names today. They were to "complete" the Aberdeen course in the following year. There were others too with the same enthusiasm for archaeology in more distant parts of the Highlands. Moidart History Society, Historic Assynt and Brora Heritage Society also celebrated their 20th birthdays in 2018.

It would be impossible to mention all the many places that have received attention over the years; a few have been selected here as examples. Most members enjoy prospecting for new archaeological sites, an activity which has gained the NOSAS name of "fossicking". Many voyages of discovery have been made visiting previously recorded sites and finding new ones - ice houses at Invershin, the broch at Torrisdale in sunshine, and recessed platforms at Loch Oich in sleet and snow.

Recording and surveying the new sites is an essential part of the prospecting process. Many new sites have been submitted to national and local archaeological databases: Canmore, and Highland Council's Historic Environment Record. One of the first sites to be surveyed using linked plane-tables was an earthwork at Achnasoul near Marybank. But some of the most memorable achievements in the early years were those of the three large landscape projects:

■ The first one, in 1999, targeted Glen Feshie in Badenoch. It seemed like a good idea after finishing the Aberdeen Course to investigate a landscape and link the archaeological sites with their history. In retrospect it was a pretty ambitious project, but many happy hours were enjoyed exploring the glen and recording the sites. The result was a gazetteer of the sites, a subsequent programme of NOSAS surveying and excavating, and a fascinating story involving the Duchess of Bedford and the Victorian painter Sir Edwin Landseer. The story of the glen was told in the first NOSAS publication: *Glen Feshie – the History and Archaeology of a Highland Glen* (Marshall 2013).

■ The second project, under the leadership of John Wombell, was part

Fig. 6: Recording recessed platforms, Loch Oich

Fig. 7: Post excavation discussions of shoreline bothy, Loch Hourn

Fig. 8: NOSAS interviewed for Landward programme, Strathconon

Fig. 9: HAF walk around illicit stills, Scatwell, Strathconon

Fig. 10: Walking the Killearnan to Kilbride/Conon road

Fig. 11: Walking the Clachan to Dundonnell road

of the nationwide SCAPE programme and based on Loch Hourn in Knoydart. Here in the 18th and 19th century there had been a thriving seasonal fishing industry described by Thomas Pennant in his tour of 1772 and depicted by William Daniel in 1819. The group explored the nooks and crannies of the dramatic landscape of Loch Hourn with the help of the estate keeper and his boat. 1300 archaeological sites were located and recorded, many of them remnants of the early fishing industry – piers, fishing stations, cleared beaches and the remains of shoreline bothies.

■ From 2006 to 2009 Strathconon, a long glen west of Dingwall, was the objective of the third project. It was part of the Scotland's Rural Past scheme, a nationwide project aimed at encouraging community groups to take an interest in their local archaeology. 1100 sites were recorded; the number indicative of the large population of 1100 documented in 1821. There were 35 townships, over 300 shielings and over 50 illicit still bothies. The number of shielings and the discovery of rentals being paid in cash as early as 1721 provided evidence of cattle being reared for export, but the remarkable number of illicit stills located revealed a people resorting to desperate measures to survive. Inevitably the walks and talks that have been made to these sites have been very popular.

There have been many other activities. In the early days some of the old Highland roads were walked – Kilbride to Killearnan and Clachan to Dundonnell, for example. Fieldwalking at Conon produced a barbed and tanged arrowhead which was adopted as the NOSAS logo. The group added their bit to conservation – on one occasion felling a tree which was threatening a kiln. The variety of skills between the group was quite surprising; not only had they a qualified tree feller but also a pilot, Jim Bone, who sadly died in June 2018, having produced many helpful aerial photographs.

Not surprisingly excavation has always been one of the most popular activities. Initially people helped with those of other organisations – Brora Salt Pans and Applecross Broch for example. But after a while the group began to run their own small scale projects – a fisher's bothy at Loch Hourn, tattie pits in Strathconon and later a kiln at the Mulchaich/Ferintosh distillery. Now of course they have embarked on the much larger project of Tarradale Through Time. Of

Fig. 12: Conservation – felling a tree threatening a kiln

Fig. 13: Excavating tattie pits in Strathconon

Fig: 14: Excavating a kiln at the site of the Mulchaich distillery

Fig. 15: The NOSAS collection at Dingwall Library

this, more elsewhere in this Yearbook. The aim of spreading the word and involving the rest of the community has been achieved by putting on walks, talks and displays highlighting NOSAS projects and activities; members have also made many contributions to the annual Highland Archaeology Festival.

In 2000 a collection of books was kindly donated by a member who was leaving the area; it became the foundation for the NOSAS library and has subsequently received many more additions finding a home in the Highland Council library at Dingwall Academy. In 2004 another milestone was achieved with the setting up of the NOSAS website (www.nosas.co.uk). This is now an active, vibrant, useful resource; most reports of past NOSAS projects are available there. The NOSAS Facebook page currently has over 1200 followers, and our periodic blog has over 80 contributions. More recently, some members have been exploring ways in which IT can help and enhance the results of projects; but this topic is discussed more thoroughly elsewhere in this publication so it is not proposed to go into it any further here.

The first 10 years saw NOSAS membership grow steadily and significantly, and despite ups and downs these numbers have remained at healthy levels ever since. There is a wealth of archaeological sites in the scenic landscape of the Highlands, but there are also so many other facets to NOSAS activities too - the fresh air, the physical and intellectual exercise and the social interaction and camaraderie of like-minded people. NOSAS has achieved much in the last twenty years; it has been a great privilege to be part of such a varied and enthusiastic bunch of people.

References

Marshall, M. (2013) *Glen Feshie: The History and Archaeology of a Highland Glen* 2nd edition. Inverness: North of Scotland Archaeological Society

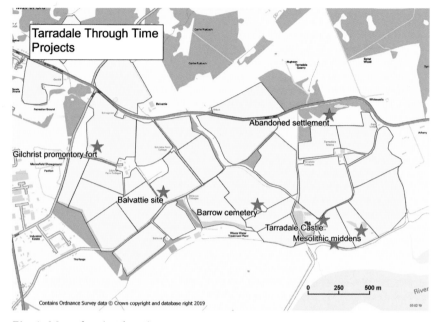

Fig: 1: Map of project locations

Fig. 2: Antler T-axe
from site 2B
© AOC Archaeology

Fig. 3: Antler harpoon or
spear from site 2B ©
AOC Archaeology

2: Tarradale Through Time
Discovering the Archaeology of the Black Isle

by Eric Grant

NOSAS succeeded in 2017 to obtain funding from the Heritage Lottery Fund for an archaeological project based in the Black Isle. *Tarradale Through Time: Community Engagement with Archaeology in the Highlands* grew out of the previous Tarradale field-walking programme where the quantity of lithic, ceramic and metal finds showed that there was a considerable amount of archaeology to be uncovered below the plough soil. The area concerned covers about 750 hectares of farmland on the north side of the Beauly Firth and immediately east of Muir of Ord.

Tarradale Through Time comprises several subprojects involving either archaeological excavation or field survey. At the time of writing, the fieldwork for five of these subprojects has been completed whilst the final subproject, an excavation of part of the Tarradale barrow cemetery, is scheduled to take place in the late summer of 2019. So far, the project has been remarkably successful, with some major discoveries. It has involved the local community, and the archaeological results have been disseminated to a wide audience through newspaper and journal articles, broadcast media, and online (eg. Grant 2018).

Subproject 1: Tarradale Castle Excavations 2017

Unexpectedly, the first subproject was the least successful in terms of adding to our knowledge of the area. In September 2017 the supposed site of a 13th century earth-and-timber castle at Tarradale was investigated. This castle is known to have existed at Tarradale until it was destroyed by Robert Bruce in 1308 (Barnes and Barrow 1970). Field-walking and metal-detecting had uncovered many finds of medieval pottery, coins and metalwork in the area where we assumed the castle lay. The topography was also very suggestive of this being the site of a motte and bailey. Although geophysical investigations had shown some promising features under the surface of the plough soil, excavation showed that these were largely natural, representing ancient stream beds that had filled up with stones and gravel. It is possible that the earthen banks and other castle features had been completely destroyed and subsequently landscaped. Therefore, although the exact location of Tarradale Castle is unresolved at present, it is intended to extend the search for the castle in the future.

Subproject 2: Shell Midden Excavations 2017

In 2011 NOSAS helped to excavate some test pits in a field at Tarradale where deeper ploughing than normal had brought a thick layer of marine shells to the surface. It became clear that under the plough soil was an extensive shell midden that included oyster, cockle, mussel and periwinkle. Radiocarbon dating of fragments of antler and charcoal that were found in the shell midden provided dates in the seventh millennium BC (hazel charcoal was dated to 6632-6480 cal BC and antler to 6204-6005 cal BC, both at 95.4% probability). These are the earliest dates for the Mesolithic in the Black Isle or Easter Ross, and firmly put Tarradale on the Mesolithic map of Scotland.

It is not known if these first Mesolithic hunters and gatherers were permanent settlers or seasonal visitors. However, the picture that is emerging is of occupation on raised beaches or estuarine terraces along the edge of the Beauly Firth, their location depending on the level of the sea at the time. Just below Tarradale House and close to the previous shoreline, part of the lowest raised beach had escaped ploughing in recent years and test pitting showed the presence of a shell midden. As part of the *Tarradale Through Time* project, in 2017 a major excavation was undertaken at this site, just below the old degraded cliff line and about 9m above the current sea level. The site, which we called site 2B, produced exciting evidence of Mesolithic occupation. Not many lithic finds were made, probably because the

Fig. 4: Shell midden site 2B, showing position of possible hut with stone settings

people were short of good quality flint and used quartz and other stone materials instead. However, we do know that they used antler and bone for making tools and other artefacts.

The excavation uncovered a large shell midden within which was an axe head made of red deer antler (Fig. 2). It is a type of axe called an antler T-axe. Although this type is well known on the continent, only three or four examples have ever been found in Scotland before (Elliott 2015). The Tarradale T-axe is well preserved and easily identifiable, with one end sharpened to make an axe blade and with a hole drilled through the middle to take a narrow shaft. Antler is very hard and quite resilient and so can be used for splitting wood and stripping bark from trees. However, these axes could also be used for digging up edible roots, cutting up seal and deer carcasses, or dismembering the occasional stranded whale. This exciting find was the first antler T-axe found in the North of Scotland. However a few days later a second axe was found and, although not in such good condition, it was still easily identifiable as another antler T-axe. Later the same day, part of an antler spear or harpoon was also discovered (Fig. 3). This is an extremely rare find and, although it was broken, it was easily recognised by archaeologists as a "biserial barbed antler point". It may have been a harpoon, i.e. a spear that is thrown with a line on the end of it to catch seals or wildfowl. Alternatively it may have been used as a thrusting spear; if a hunter was able to get close to a seal, or for stabbing salmon gathered in a fish trap.

Several organic samples found in the shell midden gave dates within the range 4782 to 3643 cal BC. This would suggest that people were living on this raised beach at Tarradale in the late Mesolithic period and continuing into the Neolithic as a separate group or possibly merging with Neolithic settlers. This site may prove to be even more important as, within the shell midden, was a silt-filled depression a few metres across (Fig. 4) which can be interpreted as the base circle for a Mesolithic hut or shelter (cf. Mithen and Wicks 2018). If this is indeed the case, then we have important evidence for Mesolithic settlement structures at Tarradale.

At the same time as the excavation of Site 2B, investigations were made at another promontory 500m further east. Several test pits and trenches provided more evidence of shell middens, suggestive of either permanent or periodic settlement over a considerable period of time. A date of 6071 to 5925 BC (at 95.4% probability) was obtained from the top of this promontory, suggesting there was an earlier period of Mesolithic settlement here. The radiocarbon dates obtained from the other test pits and trenches were more in keeping with those from Site 2B, being in the range between 4352 and 3961 BC. There was also one later date of 3012 - 2895 BC, well into the Neolithic period, suggesting that either the tradition of Mesolithic hunting and gathering continued, or that Neolithic farmers were happy to continue exploiting the rich shellfish resources of the estuary.

Subproject 3: Survey and Excavation of an Abandoned Settlement 2018

There are a number of ruined and abandoned cottages on the edges of fields in the Tarradale area. One subproject, designed to be a relatively simple exercise, was to locate and accurately survey a group of houses c. 200 to 250 years old. Archaeology, however, is never straightforward, and our investigations provided an unexpected mystery.

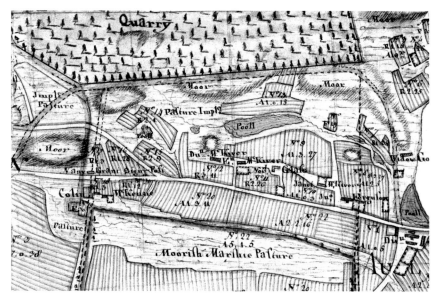

Fig. 5: Mailers' houses on the 1788 Aitken map (reproduced with permission)

In the 1780s Dr Kenneth Murchison, the owner of Tarradale, commissioned the surveyor David Aitken to map the whole estate with the intention of instigating agricultural improvements (Grant and Mutch 2015). The resultant 1788 map (which is in private ownership) is a detailed document showing fields made up of parcels of rig and furrow, some clearly associated with smallholdings. Superimposed on top of these are outlines of bigger fields about to be created for enlarged and improved farms. Aitken's map describes a group of holdings to the north of Tarradale Mains Farm, "in 19 separate fields, possessed by 11 mailers" (Fig. 5). The map helpfully gave us the names of all the tenants, although none of these names could be identified in a rental list of Tarradale mailers dated 1791. It could be that the 1791 rental does not list the mailers in our area but instead concentrates on the upwards of 50 tenants who had small plots of land further north in the area now known as Muir of Tarradale. Alternatively, the settlement might have been abandoned by 1791 which raises the question of why the occupants left.

The proposed agricultural improvements indicated by the 1788 map and the building of the new Tarradale Mains farm in the early

1790s may have been important in the movement or relocation of the tenants. By the time of the first census in 1841 the settlement was gone, and it is not shown at all on the 1st edition Ordnance Survey map of 1872. A further complication was that the 1788 map clearly shows five tenants' houses in the specific area we were investigating, whereas remains of six houses were found on the ground. Four of these were located exactly where we expected to find them according to the map, however the remains of a fifth house was found just to the west of its expected position, and we also found a range of separate outbuildings not recorded on the map. To add further to our difficulty, we then found an additional larger and well-built house to the west of the other cottages on what is shown as arable land on the 1788 map.

The houses we uncovered were about 16m long by 5m wide and roughly orientated east-west. They appear to have had one or two main rooms with 'outshots' or smaller attached buildings, probably housing animals or storage. The houses all have stone foundations, but there was insufficient stone lying around to suggest that the walls had been built entirely of stone. This led us to consider whether the houses were built of turf or clay set on a low foundation of stones and with a turf or thatched roof. Parallels for turf walled houses can be seen from the reconstructed buildings at the Highland Folk Museum at Newtonmore. Clay walled houses built on stone plinths were also a common feature in the Highlands, although few of these survive today; clay houses are discussed more widely by Walker, McGregor and Little (1996).

The most visible structure in the landscape we named House 2 (Fig. 6), described as belonging to Duncan McKiver on the 1788 map. The lower front wall, although constructed with relatively small stones, was well built and bonded with clay, while the back wall was very ruinous. So far, our evidence has not led to a definite conclusion whether the house was built wholly of clay above the scanty stone foundations, or of clay and/or turf. However, the considerable amount of clay we discovered suggested that this played an important part in the construction of these buildings, rather than them being built completely of stone as we would tend to expect for cottages in the Highlands.

Fig. 6: House 2 appearing through the dead bracken

Excavation of a small area in the interior of House 2 revealed a clay floor. We also found several fragments of cast iron cooking pots around the site, perhaps representing the end of the use of the site when broken articles were abandoned as the tenants left for better opportunities elsewhere. However, we found very few pieces of pottery suggesting that, either the inhabitants were too poor to afford them, or else they took their precious ceramics with them.

What started as the straightforward recording of buildings on the 1788 map was followed by some confusion in relating the houses on the ground to those on the map. We concluded that, although the 1788 map is probably accurate, it represents a snapshot in time, whilst we were seeing the remains of a multi-period landscape with houses of different ages. The two additional houses we found perhaps represent a later reoccupation of the site connected with the development of the nearby Tarradale quarry.

Subproject 4: Gilchrist Promontory Fort Excavation 2018

In September 2018 two sites were investigated; a fortified enclosure just west of Gilchrist church and a rather enigmatic and possibly ritual site south of Gilchrist church, located on Balvattie Farm. The Gilchrist fort is a rather unobtrusive monument and walking past it gives no clue to its existence, size or age. Canmore describes it as a promontory fort based on their interpretation of crop marks. These show three arcs, possibly ditches, "apparently designed to cut off approach to a tongue of low-lying and comparatively level ground running NW into marshland. They are in effect part of the defensive system of a promontory fort measuring about 85m by 30m" (Canmore ID 12690).

In addition to the black-and-white photographs on the Canmore database, the late Jim Bone, a pilot and an enthusiastic archaeologist, took colour photographs of the site, one of which (Fig. 7) shows three dark green curved features representing the fort's ditches on the east side of the promontory. The ditches are now under cultivation and have been filled in and ploughed flat so there is nothing to see above ground; it is only the aerial photographs that have enabled archaeologists to see this as a fortified promontory. It is unusual to find a promontory fort inland unless it is in a situation like this where it is surrounded by water or marshland. Most hill and promontory forts in Scotland appear to have been constructed during the late Bronze Age and Iron Age, and the latest ones were built or reoccupied in Pictish times (Lock and Ralston 2017).

Our research agenda sought to identify and characterise the ditches, and to ascertain when the fort was constructed, how long it was occupied and what activities may have taken place there.

Three large trenches were initially opened. In the first trench we quickly established that the three ditches seen on aerial photographs did exist (Fig. 8), with a hint of a fourth ditch closer into the fort. The outermost ditch was reasonably shallow, but the second ditch was a massive construction 5-6m wide at the top and sloping steeply to about 1.5m below the plough soil. We consider that the upper parts of all the ditches have been lost due to ploughing and the intervening banks of excavated material flattened. The third innermost ditch was less deep, and right on the edge of the actual fort area we found what may be the fourth and innermost ditch. This might have continued round the fort perimeter as a wall, perhaps with a timber fence or pal-

Fig. 7: Aerial photograph of Gilchrist showing ditches as dark green curves
© *The JS Bone Collection*

isade at the top or just in front. The bigger ditches had been filled in with large boulders, probably field clearance in the medieval period, as medieval pottery was found in the ditch fills.

The scale of the defences was impressive and clearly represented a major construction involving a huge amount of labour. It is easy to see these forts simply as defensive structures with permanent or intermittent occupation, but they can also be viewed as symbols of power for the local elite who could assemble their followers during times of unrest or use the fort interior as a place of assembly for civil gatherings and ritual activities.

A trench that we dug from the interior of the site northwards across the long side of the promontory into the bog proved to be particularly interesting (Fig. 9). As we excavated northwards towards the bog we encountered the remains of what could have been a wall running along the side of the promontory; beyond that the ground dropped very steeply. We found pieces of timber which could just be the remains of trees but were possibly part of structures such as a palisade fence associated with the fort. However, trapped within the remains of the supposed perimeter wall were some pieces of pottery and part of a rotary quern. These could represent rubbish thrown over the side of the fort towards the marsh. The pottery is fragmentary but very thick and quite crudely made by hand. We are currently waiting to have this pottery analysed as it may give us a good indication of the date of use of the fort. Another trench on the highest part of the fort showed furrows at the base of the topsoil representing old plough marks. It is likely that ploughing activity has destroyed any structural evidence in this area, and much of the soil has drifted downhill.

In a trench further to the west, we found a spread of clay just under the topsoil, too regular and straight sided to be a natural deposit. It may be the floor of a building within the fort that has survived because it is further down the promontory and away from the areas that were more intensively ploughed. Right on the clay floor we found a small piece of pottery, possibly part of a crucible, suggesting small-scale metalworking was being carried out on the site. There is much post excavation analysis to be done, but the very least we can say at present is that somebody important was living at Gilchrist around two to three thousand years ago who had sufficient power to encourage his (or her) followers to construct what we now know to be a significant defensive feature.

Subproject 5: Balvattie Excavations 2018

The second site excavated in September 2018, lying about 350m south-east of Gilchrist church on Balvattie Farm, was very different. It was also identified from aerial photographs which show a circular feature, with arc-shaped features, and some linear patterns (Fig. 10). The circular feature superficially looked like a roundhouse although it seemed too large (26 to 30m) for this. At the time of writing, the Canmore website simply describes these features as an enclosure of unassigned period (Canmore ID 12685). Our excavations show that the site is a large and complex one, likely to date from the prehistoric period. Trench 3 picked up the circular feature precisely (Fig. 11), revealing a ditch about 2m wide and up to 1m deep, although the upper part of the ditch had been destroyed by ploughing leaving no indication of it on the surface.

Fig. 8 (above): Long section showing sequence of fort ditches under excavation

Fig. 9 (right): Excavated trench running from side of fort into the peat, showing degraded possible perimeter wall

There was much evidence of intensive burning within the area enclosed by the circular ditch, although apart from a few pieces of charcoal and some tiny pieces of bone there was no indication of what the purpose of the burning had been. Outside the ditched enclosure were a number of pits c. 1m wide by 0.5m deep (originally probably twice as deep). These pits may initially have had large posts with stones packed round the base, but it appears that they are not simple post holes as small pieces of pottery were carefully deposited in these pits. Similar pits dating from the Neolithic have been found elsewhere in Scotland (Brophy and Noble 2012), but until scientific results are obtained we are unable to say how old these pits are and what their function was. A very large pit, which stood out as a prominent lush mark on aerial photographs, was also excavated (Trench 4). The upper levels contained dumped field gathered stones and showed much evidence of burning, but the original 2m deep pit may have been a naturally formed hole that filled up with slope-washed coarse sand and gravel and was levelled off much later.

Trench 6 picked up one of the curved features seen on aerial photographs. This was a well-constructed, narrow, and straight-sided ditch, ending with a distinct terminal feature and an adjacent post hole. A tentative interpretation is that it may have been a ditch or slot for a wooden palisade with a gap for an entrance or gateway and an additional post for strength. The linear features seen on aerial photographs may represent paths running through the entrance way to the inner circular enclosure. These features may not all be the same age, although they are likely to be later prehistoric. There is no suggestion that the site at Balvattie was defensive in the way that the fort at Gilchrist appears to have been, although its size does again suggest a complex social order.

Over the last two years, the *Tarradale Through Time* excavations have uncovered significant archaeological remains, indicating multi-period exploitation of the land over several thousand years. What has been discovered so far suggests that the wider Muir of Ord area was extremely important in the past and of increasing significance in relation to what we know about the archaeology of the Highlands.

More information about the *Tarradale Through Time* project can be found online at www.tarradalethroughtime.co.uk.

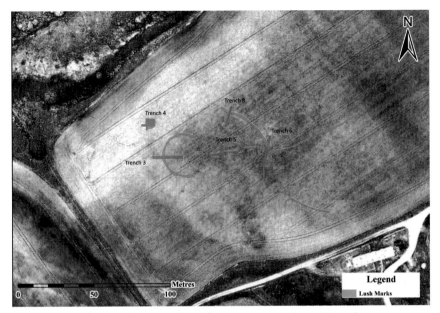

Fig. 10: Plan of Balvattie excavations showing crop marks and trenches
© Highland Archaeological Services

References

Barnes, P. and Barrow, G. (1970) 'The Movements of Robert Bruce between September 1307 and May 1308'. *The Scottish Historical Review*, 49 (1), 46-59

Brophy K. and Noble, G. (2012) 'Within and beyond pits: the position in lowland Neolithic Scotland'. In *Regional perspectives on Neolithic pit deposition: beyond the mundane* (Neolithic studies group seminar papers 12) ed. by Anderson-Whymark, H. and Thomas, J. Oxford: Oxbow

Elliott, B. (2015) 'Facing the Chop: Redefining British Antler Mattocks to Consider Larger-scale Maritime Networks in the Early Fifth Millennium Cal BC'. *European Journal of Archaeology*, 18 (2), 222-244

Grant, E. and Mutch, A. (2015) 'Indian Wealth and Agricultural Improvement in Northern Scotland'. *Journal of Scottish Historical Studies*, 35 (1), 25-44

Grant, E. (2018) 'Exciting discoveries on the Black Isle'. *History Scotland*, 18 (4), 10-13

Lock, G. and Ralston, I. (2017) *Atlas of hillforts of Britain and Ireland* (online). Available from <https://hillforts.arch.ox.ac.uk>

Mithen, S. and Wicks K. (2018) 'The interpretation of Mesolithic structures in Britain: new evidence from Criet Dubh, Isle of Mull, & alternative approaches to chronological analysis for inferring occupation tempos & settlement patterns'. *Proceedings of the Prehistoric Society*, 84, 77-110

Walker, B., McGregor, C. and Little R. (1996) *Earth structures and construction in Scotland: a guide to the recognition and conservation of earth technology in Scottish buildings.* Edinburgh: Historic Scotland

Fig. 11: Trench 3, showing line of circular ditch (middle of picture) with burnt area beyond and pits in foreground

3: Torvean Fort
A Neglected Monument on the Edge of Inverness

by Jonathan Wordsworth

Lying less than two kilometres south-west from the centre of Inverness, Torvean hillfort is a neglected scheduled monument (SM3806) of national importance, situated on the edge of the former Torvean quarry and currently obscured by mature woodland, scrub and rough vegetation. It is also suffering from persistent trail bike damage that is causing erosion to the fabric of the monument.

Centred at NH 6437 4315, the fort is on one of a series of periglacial ridges that are considered nationally important, forming part of the extensive Torvean Landforms SSSI 1557. The JNCC statement for the site describes it as "notable for glacial geomorphology, containing an outstanding range of landforms and deposits formed by the meltwaters of the last (Late Devensian) ice-sheet, between approximately 14,000 and 13,000 years ago [...] it contains what is believed to be the

Fig. 1: 1991 aerial photograph of Torvean Quarry, adjacent to the Caledonian Canal and River Ness, after its closure in 1989. The fort can be seen in top right as a wooded feature above the upper line of pylons © JS Bone Collection

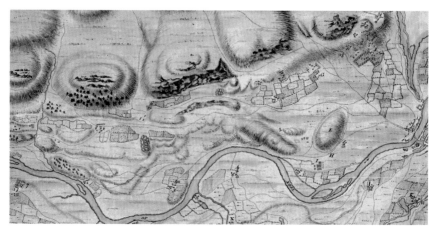

Fig. 2: Detail from Bastide's map: A General Survey of Inverness and country adjoining to the foot of Loch Ness c. 1725. Reproduced with the permission of the National Library of Scotland

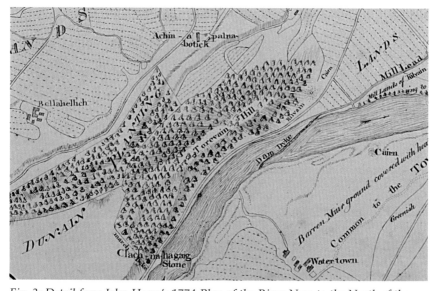

Fig. 3: Detail from John Home's 1774 Plan of the River Ness to the North of the bridge of Inverness © Inverness Museum. More 18th century plans of this area can be seen at the National Records of Scotland: RHP671, RHP2505, RHP35947 & RHP46298

highest esker in Britain, with a height of over 68m" (Joint Nature Conservation Committee 2019).

The area immediately to the east of the fort has been extensively quarried for sand and gravel and though this quarry closed in 1989, the morphology of the area has been severely altered. The quarry lies outside the immediate environs of the fort, but the excavations and dumps from these works have affected the situation of this monument.

Unlike Craig Phadrig to the north which has long been recorded, Torvean hillfort was not shown on the earliest maps of the area, such as Bastide's 1725 map. On Roy's Military Survey of c.1750 it is shown as an undifferentiated treeless ridge to the west of Tomnahurich.

Ignorance of the Torvean monument is continued in a fine series of later maps held in the National Archives of Scotland. These relate to a long standing dispute concerning the rights to catch salmon in the River Ness. Dating from 1765 onwards these maps show Torvean as a single ridge. The best of these, John Home's plan of 1774, shows the ridge as now obscured by a plantation of trees. The ridge and fort have been largely wooded ever since.

The Home map is also important for showing the location of a substantial cairn at Kilvain (Torvean), later destroyed during the construction of the Caledonian Canal, where an important and substantial Pictish silver chain was recovered in 1808. It was recorded in the 1st Statistical Account for Inverness and Bona Parish of 1791 that "there is a very large cairn near the river at the foot of a hill called Torvean. It some years ago was partly removed, a coffin was found composed of six thick flags" (Rose, Watson and Fraser 1793). This may be the remains of a burial of prehistoric date. Alternatively, it could be the resting place of a Pictish ruler, perhaps resident before his or her death at Torvean Fort.

Torvean Fort (or indeed the cairn) is not shown, for example, on the detailed 1804 plan (Fig. 4) by George Brown showing the projected line of the land to be removed for the Caledonian Canal. Nor was it shown on the 1st edition Ordnance Survey maps of the area, surveyed in 1868-70. The Torvean ridge seems to have been largely under woodland for 250 years.

The fort was first described in the *Transactions of Inverness Scientific*

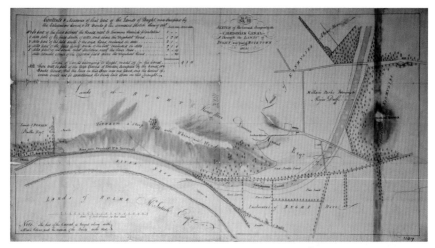

Fig. 4: Hill of Torvain, as marked on George Brown's 1804 Sketch of the ground occupied by the Caledonian Canal through the lands of Bught, and part of Muirtown. RHP 1107 Contains NRS data © Crown copyright

Fig. 5: Torvean on the 1st edition Ordnance Survey map, surveyed 1868-70. Reproduced with the permission of the National Library of Scotland

TORVEAN AND THE VALLEY OF THE NESS
FROM THE DISTRICT ASYLUM APPROACH

Fig. 6: View of Torvean ridge and fort viewed from Craig Dunain. Note Tomnahurich Hill behind centre left (ISSFC 1885)

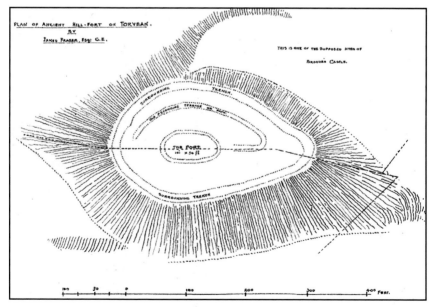

Fig. 7: Plan of Torvean hillfort, drawn by James Fraser for Inverness Scientific Society and Field Club. (ISSFC 1885: 265)

Society and Field Club (now Inverness Field Club) following an excursion led by Dr. Aitken in September 1879 (ISSFC 1885: 259-265). It is possible that by the time of their visit the trees shown in the earlier OS survey had been felled, depending on how one reads the picture in Fig. 6.

The sketch plan above (Fig. 7) is not a fully accurate depiction, as there is currently no sign of a rampart or perimeter bank on the summit and the line of the upper ditch does not correspond to the topography on the ground. Note the line of the plantation boundary line running down the centre of the fort. An additional description of the site was drawn up following a further excursion by the Society in July 1917:

It is of oval form, 100 feet long and 50 feet wide, protected by a surrounding trench at a considerable lower level in the slopes of the hill, forming an irregular oval, 340 feet long and 200 feet wide. On the north side is seen another, intermediate between the outer trench and the top, which has a gradual ascent towards the east end, where the access to the top is easiest. (ISSFC 1917: 377).

Despite revisions to the OS maps in 1892, 1902, 1929, 1950 and 1955-59, it was not until 1962 (see Fig. 8) that the fort was accurately depicted on OS maps, following a survey at 1:2500 and a description by an OS Archaeological Field Investigator "WDJ" in 1960 (Canmore). It was this survey that led to it being scheduled as an Ancient Monument of National Importance in 1964.

Note that no planting is shown on the monument at this time, that a mast is recorded on the centre of the monument, and that a pylon and associated power line have been inserted to the east. It is possible that the site lay unforested for a number of years before this, as a land utilisation survey undertaken in the mid-1930s suggests it was also not a plantation at that time (National Library of Scotland). There may have been individual trees growing on the fort, such as the now large ash tree on the south east corner.

The current conifer plantations on the north and northwest of the fort were established in 1963, according to estate records. Trees were not however planted in the interior or the south side of the fort.

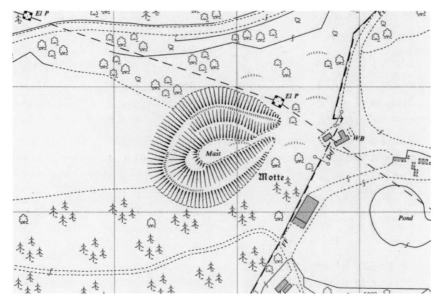

Fig. 8: Detail from OS Plan NH6443-NH6543, surveyed in 1962, recording the fort for the first time. Reproduced with the permission of the National Library of Scotland

Subsequent natural regeneration, and the growth of gorse and bracken, mean that the outline of the fort is now obscured and therefore not known to most inhabitants of Inverness.

Though described as a Motte (a form of site likely to date from after the 11th century AD) on both the 1962 OS plan and on the Scheduled Monument documentation, the fort is no longer listed as such in either the Highland Council or the Historic Environment Scotland records for this site. On morphological grounds, the fort could be of any date from Iron Age to medieval, though the proximity to the Kilvain cairn containing the early silver chain does at least raise the possibility that it was constructed for a Pictish chieftain, perhaps even King Bridei, as suggested by Dr Aitken in 1879. As no excavation has taken place on this site and any archaeological deposits are likely to be compromised by the series of tree crops and other developments on the summit, this may never be answered.

The topography of the fort can be best seen from the terrain models derived from Scottish government lidar data (Figs. 9 and 10). The terrain was scanned at 1m accuracy. It gives both a good view of the topography of the fort and the quarried out-parts of the Torvean Ridge.

Following the closure of the quarry, in which substantial quantities of sand and gravel had been removed, the area has lain derelict. This is despite various schemes promoted by Highland Council and the Inverness Burgh Common Good Fund, the latter being the recipient of the rents for the material extracted by the quarry owners. The proposed schemes have included the construction of a dry ski slope facility. In 2016 a local MSP, John Finnie, proposed that it should be formally adopted as a trail bike track. This has been informally happening for some years and more recently trail bikes have been using the ready access to the quarry to extend routes over the footprint of the fort. This is causing problems of erosion as well as discouraging public access to the fort.

The summit of the fort is primarily covered in coarse grassland with substantial areas of gorse scrub and bracken and a single sycamore tree in the centre. This has been used for a campsite with a large scaffolding pole, metal pegs inserted into the tree trunk, and a substantial fireplace formed of stones and ash. On the north and west slopes of the fort is a dense plantation of conifers, mostly hybrid larch with some scots pine planted in 1963; whilst on the south and east are predominantly mixed broadwoods, mostly sycamore, but including oak, ash, birch, cherry and beech. Much of this is probably self-seeded. The most prominent morphological feature on the summit is a rounded earthen bank c. 0.3m high by c. 0.4m wide and supporting a now derelict post and wire fence. There is also one large ash tree, possibly residual from an earlier planting, with several stumps of earlier trees c. 0.4m diameter still being visible along the line of the southern boundary ditch. There is also a mixed tangle of oak, gean, hazel and elder visible along the eastern edge before coming to the cleared tract down the line of the pylon corridor which is now predominantly covered in bracken.

Due to current tree cover and rank vegetation, the plan in Fig. 11 can only be seen as an approximate measured survey of the fort as currently surviving. The fort does not lie in council ownership, belonging instead to Dochfour Estate. However, the trail bike tracks

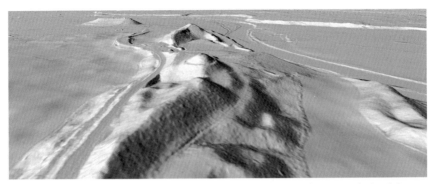

Fig. 9: Contour plan and terrain models of Torvean Fort and quarry, derived from lidar data, in relation to the A92, the Caledonian Canal, the River Ness and the remnant Torvean glacial ridge © Alan Thompson

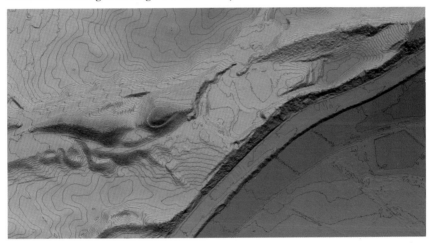

Fig. 10: Terrain models of Torvean Fort and quarry, derived from lidar data © Alan Thompson

do not respect this boundary and no fence line was restored between the council-owned land and the estate when the quarry was in operation or after it closed. The writer has noted an increasing number of tracks used and depth of eroded ground caused by the bikes on this site in the past year. Bikers use the site at all times of the year.

Visits by the Historic Scotland Monument Warden in 1992, 1994, 1998 and 2007 had recorded neither camping nor bike damage to the site, so this is a recent but worsening problem. The writer has approached the estate, Historic Environment Scotland and Highland

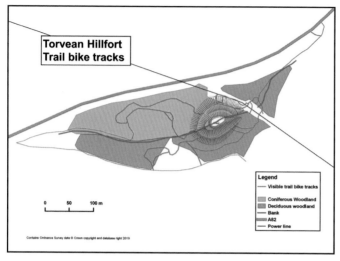

Torvean Hillfort
Trail bike tracks

Legend
— Visible trail bike tracks
Coniferous Woodland
Deciduous woodland
— Bank
A82
— Power line

0   50   100 m

Contains Ordnance Survey data © Crown copyright and database right 2019

Fig. 11: GPS plan of current Trail Bike tracks around Torvean Fort. © Bob Jones

Fig. 12: A typical example of trail bike erosion of the fort rampart, here on its north side. March 2018

Council in efforts to address this and it is hoped that these issues will ultimately be resolved, so that Torvean Fort will once more become a prominent and valued feature in the Inverness landscape.

Acknowledgements

I would like to thank Alan Thomson of NOSAS for processing the lidar data from the Scottish Remote Sensing Data portal (https://remotesensingdata.gov.scot/) and thereby producing the excellent terrain models of Torvean shown in Figs. 9 and 10, and Bob and Rosemary Jones, also of NOSAS, for producing the GPS plan of the trail bike tracks around the fort, as illustrated in Fig. 11.

References

Canmore (2019) *Archaeology Notes. Event ID 661708* (online). Available at <https://canmore.org.uk/event/661708>

ISSFC (1885) *Transactions of the Inverness Scientific Society and Field Club* 1885 (1), 258. Inverness: ISSFC

ISSFC (1917) *Transactions of the Inverness Scientific Society and Field Club* 1917 (8), 377. Inverness: ISSFC

Joint Nature Conservation Committee (2019) *Torvean (Quarternary of Scotland)* (online). Available at <http://jncc.defra.gov.uk/default.aspx?page=4174&gcr=1884>

National Library of Scotland (2019) *Land Utilisation Survey 1931-35 Sheet 37 Inverness* (online). Available at <https://maps.nls.uk/view/74425136>

Rose R., Watson G. and Fraser A. (1793) *Statistical Accounts of Scotland 1791-1845. Inverness, County of Inverness, OSA, Vol. IX, 1793* (online) Available at <https://tinyurl.com/yyvqrc6q>

Figs. 13 & 14. Two images of the silver chain (HC HER MHG3749) recovered from Torvean Cairn in 1807. At 2.88 kilograms it is the heaviest of ten similar chains thought to be made from Roman silver and dating to the Pictish period, possibly as early as the 5th century AD © National Museums of Scotland

Fig: 1: Gruinard Island from the mainland

Fig. 2 (left): Roy Map 1747
Isle Grunord
© British Library Board

Fig. 3: Peter May 1756 "Plan of
Little Gruinard, etc". Crown
copyright, National Records of
Scotland, RHP3401

4: A Survey of Gruinard Island

by Anne MacInnes

Gruinard Island is located within Gruinard Bay in the Parish of Loch Broom, Wester Ross and measures roughly 2 by 1km. The highest point is An Eilid at 106m. It has not been grazed for many years so is extremely overgrown with heather, bracken and rough grass. There is an area of improved land and settlement along the SE shore, although the last occupants left in the 1920s. The island achieved worldwide notoriety during the Second World War when it was used for testing of the best method for dispersal of a biological agent, in this case the anthrax bacillus, for the purposes of biological warfare. For over 40 years the island remained too badly contaminated and was quarantined, becoming known as "Anthrax Island" (BBC News 2001). In 1986 a plan was formulated to restore it back to civilian use. However, it was not until 1990 that it was declared safe and the warning notices were taken down.

Recently, enthusiasts from Gairloch Heritage Museum researched the history of the island. In conjunction with this research an archae-

Fig. 4: Approaching the SE aspect of the island, showing rig and dykes

ological survey was undertaken in early 2018 by NOSAS member Anne MacInnes with colleagues from the museum. A copy of the full report of the project, including comprehensive archive research and an account of the anthrax experiments, can be viewed in the NOSAS section of Dingwall Library.

Gruinard is derived from the Old Norse language *groenn fjoror* meaning "green firth". The name has had several variations: Gruynorde, Ellan Gruinord, Grumorta, Greinord and Isle Greenyard. Although the 1654 Blaeu map of Scotland identifies Gruinard Island, it is only with Roy's Military Map of 1747 that any detail is shown. It shows a group of buildings in the SE quarter of the island, together with associated cultivation lines.

A surveyed map by Peter May in 1756 shows the island in two parts: the north part (at the bottom!) belonging to Mackenzie of Dundonald and the south belonging to Little Gruynard Farm, which is opposite the island on the mainland. The north-south divide is still evident today. The map shows cultivation on the island, with the comment: "That part of Island Gruynard belonging to Little Gruynard is the best part of the farm, there is some good Cornfields upon it and the pasture is likewise good only that having Firth to cross makes it more inconvenient" (May 1756). He describes ridge and furrow cultivation and the fishing, which was then subject to a dispute. The letting for kelp-harvesting on the island was advertised in 1799 (Caledonian Mercury 1799).

There has been no formal archaeological investigation on the island, so the date of first settlement is unknown. However, aerial photos do show a probable roundhouse with associated enclosure and clearance piles at NG 94470 94972 on the NE corner of the island, suggesting prehistoric use. Access difficulties make it difficult to substantiate these aerial findings. There are prehistoric roundhouses, however, on nearby Isle Ewe and on the neighbouring mainland.

From the Lochbroom Militia lists, 1798-1827, and the 1888 census record of six persons on the island, the main occupants in the 19th century seem to have been cottars and fishermen. Local knowledge suggests that the island has been uninhabited since the 1920s.

The 1st edition OS map of 1875, shows evidence of field boundaries, and some buildings. In addition, Watson in his book *Place Names*

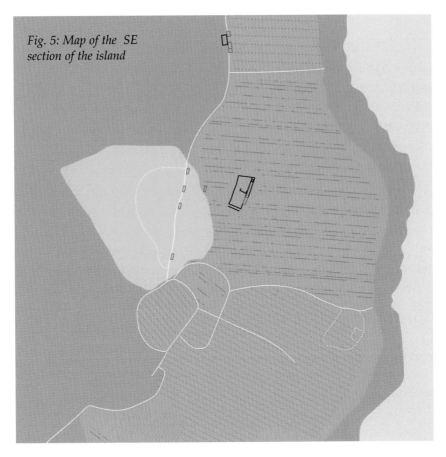

Fig. 5: Map of the SE section of the island

of Ross and Cromarty (2008) describes an ancient burial ground called Cladh Pris, the burial place of the bush or copse, at the island's SE landing place. Oral history tells of people from "up the glen" bringing their dead to Gruinard Island for burial to avoid the bodies being scavenged by predators. One of the specific aims of the survey was to find this now overgrown cemetery.

The 2018 Gruinard Island Survey

The aims of the survey carried out for Gairloch Heritage Museum in early 2018 were to identify, survey and then record what remained on the island. This proved to be difficult as the island is covered with

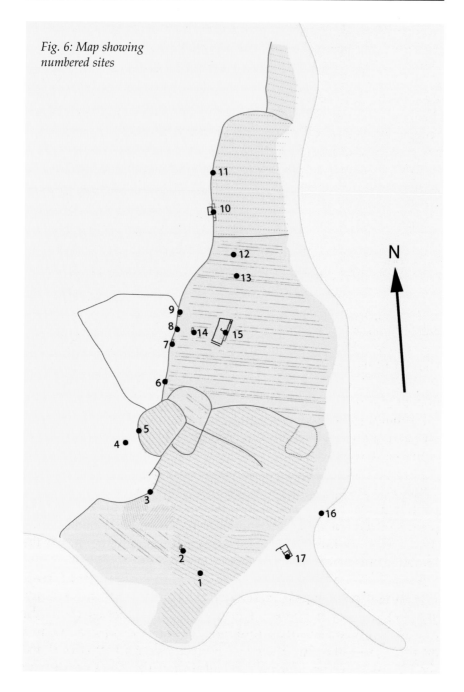

Fig. 6: Map showing numbered sites

deep moss and rank heather and grass. Several attempts were made however, leading to some success as the site accounts that follow demonstrate.

On first sailing to the island the narrow and broad rig was clearly seen; evidence of cultivation in the SE of the island. These drainage channels between the parallel banks of arable cultivation have become blocked and overgrown with deep moss. However, footings and ruins of buildings as well as stone dykes were eventually identified on the island, despite the excessive vegetation, with the probability of other features buried beneath the moss in areas considered too dangerous or difficult to investigate.

The map in Fig. 5 shows the improved area clearly, with the dykes marked out. A head dyke, which would have separated the cultivated area from grazing livestock, can still be seen and we found that most of the footings of buildings were situated adjacent to this head dyke. The discoloured area just outside and to the NW of the head dyke is the area treated with anthrax and subsequently decontaminated with formaldehyde.

The stone dykes were followed and surveyed, and 18 other sites were identified and recorded. Fourteen of these were either footings or ruins of buildings, as shown and numbered in Fig. 6. Drone photography provided clear images of all the sites from a lower altitude.

The buildings included stone and turf footings (site no. 2), the footings of a substantial building constructed with large rough boulders with two compartments (no. 6, Fig. 7), and the more substantial ruins of site nos. 9, 10, 14, 15 and 17.

Site no. 9 is shown as unroofed on the 1st edition OS map and comprises the thickly vegetated footings of two adjoining buildings. The walls have an inner and outer facing and are made with small boulders. It was difficult to establish features like entrances due to the tumbled nature of the ruins and vegetation cover.

Site no. 10 is also shown as unroofed on the 1st edition OS map, with ruins of what appear to be a barn or byre with a central unroofed area adjoined by a house. There is a midden downslope of the barn/byre and an enclosure upslope. The walls are upstanding to a maximum height of 2m. The house was constructed with chosen and shaped stones which are coursed and watertight. The barn or byre

Fig. 7: Surveying the building at site no. 6

Fig. 8: Ruined House, site no. 15

Fig. 9: Shepherd's Bothy, site no. 17

Fig. 10: Drone photograph, site no. 17

Fig. 11: Site no. 15

was a phased building of rougher construction with rounded inner corners and two entrances.

Site no. 14 is also shown as unroofed on the 1st edition OS map, comprising the ruined footings of three adjoining buildings. They are roughly constructed with chosen stone and boulders.

Site no. 15 (Figs. 8 & 11) comprises the ruins of a house, unroofed on the 1st edition OS map, and a walled enclosure. The house walls are coursed, with snecking and mortar between the boulders, upstanding to a maximum height of 2.2m. Its rear wall is set into the bank of the enclosure which is at a higher level upslope from the house and outbuildings. The rectangular walled enclosure has out-buildings built along three sides and constructed with rough stones and boulders to a maximum height of 1.6m.

Site no. 17 (Figs. 9 & 10) is the ruin of a known shepherd's bothy with adjoining fank and dipper. It was used by the MOD during the anthrax experiments, and now has lime mortar and cement skews applied over the coursed stone construction. The gable ends stand to a height of 2.8m. The bothy is situated beside the shingle spit which is the main point of access to the island.

As well as the dykes and buildings, a slipway (site no. 16) and an associated burial ground were also identified. Both of these were mentioned by Watson (2008).

Studying the drone aerial photos, it was noticed that there was a small enclosure beside a wall where there were no cultivation rigs. This was also at the edge of a copse and just upslope from the land-ing slipway. Investigation found a ruined, heavily overgrown, stone dyke enclosing an area measuring 9 by 14m. On probing, and remov-ing some of the moss, about a dozen stones were found, placed at reg-ular intervals. Four were in a row parallel to the boundary wall. The stones were also carefully chosen, not just cobbles off the beach. There was quartzite, mica schist, patterned sandstone, and a stone with quartzite nodules included through it. No engravings were found on the stones, but this is not unusual. It was concluded that this was the burial ground.

There are animal tracks running in front of the shepherd's bothy (Fig. 9) from either otter or, more probably, invasive mink. Sadly, these animals have decimated the seabird population, so that steps are now being taken to try and eradicate the mink as has been done recently on the adjacent mainland (Wester Ross Fisheries Trust 2013).

In 1942 the, by then, uninhabited island was requisitioned by the Ministry of Supply of the UK Government for germ warfare experiments. The price of £500 was paid. The island was contaminated with anthrax bacteria and remained too badly contaminated for over 40 years to allow any unauthorised access (Szasz 1995). Warning notices were placed both on the island and neighbouring mainland. In 1986 plans were made to decontaminate the island which was first burnt and then treated with formaldehyde. It was finally declared safe in 1990 and repurchased by the heirs of the original owner for £500. Video footage of the anthrax experiments is available from Rankin (2019).

A plaque and metal tripod with granite block suspended below it was placed on the island by Scottish social sculptor George Wyllie (1921-2012). Sadly, this was not found during the survey. Apparently, beneath the structure was a plaque that read 'For air, stone, and the equilibrium of understanding'. Underneath that smaller writing stated 'Welcome Back Gruinard' and 'George Wyllie and Murray Grigor, April 1990'.

Conclusion

The discovery of the previously unrecorded burial ground was perhaps the high point of the survey. The remains of the buildings, walls and enclosures provide memories of an island population which by its very nature had to be self-sufficient. It seems there was, for a time, a thriving community on Gruinard Island, like many other islands on the West Coast. There is something attractive and special about visiting islands. For the last 50 years this island has been out of bounds; now we are able to experience it again for ourselves. 'Welcome Back Gruinard', indeed.

Acknowledgements

Thanks to members of the project team for permission to use their photos, to Jane Macintyre for her archive research and to Hugh

Macintyre for providing and skippering the boat which ferried the survey team (Anne MacInnes, Gordon Grant, Jim and Karen Buchanan).

References

BBC News (2001) *Living with Anthrax Island* (online). Available at: <http://news.bbc.co.uk/1/hi/uk/1643031.stm>

Caledonian Mercury (1799) *KELP TO BE LET* (online). Available at: <https://tinyurl.com/y5aek3jq>

May, P. (1756) *Plan of Little Gruinard, Loch Broom, Ross and Cromarty* (online). Available at <https://tinyurl.com/yywapx8d>

Rankin, A. (2019) *Gruinard Island Loch Broom* (online). Available at: <http://scotislands.com/gruinard-island-loch-broom>

Fig. 12: George Wyllie with his sculpture, 1990 © BBC

Szasz, M. (1995) 'The Impact of World War II on the Land: Gruinard Island, Scotland, and Trinity Site, New Mexico'. *Environmental History Review*, 19 (4), 15-30

Watson, W. (2008) *Place Names of Ross and Cromarty*. Alcester: Read Books

Wester Ross Fisheries Trust (2013) *Breeding seabirds threatened by invasive mink on nesting islands around Wester Ross* (online) Available at: <https://www.wrft.org.uk/news/newsitem.cfm?id=171>

Fig. 3: Most of the poles had step-irons

Fig. 1: The telephone poles can be seen alongside the estate road looking NE

Fig. 4: Most had identifying numerals

Fig. 2: A single pole showing all the features. Looking SW

5: A Lonely Linear Line of Communication

by Meryl Marshall

In the remote hills to the south of Scatwell in Strathconon a line of derelict telephone poles marches over the hill towards Loch Orrin. They are an unusual feature at an altitude of between 330m and 430m. What was their purpose? When were they erected?

Lines of telephone poles are often thought of by some people as a blight on the landscape. However, fewer are seen nowadays and they are rapidly becoming a "thing of the past". Some might argue that they are not of archaeological importance. However, they have certainly been a part of our heritage.

These poles are located 4km south of Scatwell House. They stretch for about 1.5km from Loch an Fheoir (NH 3939 5326) at the NE end to Loch Aradaidh (NH 3862 5255) in the SW, following the line of the well-made estate track from Scatwell over to Glen Orrin. Ten disused poles in various states of preservation are seen; most are upright but some have fallen and others are at jaunty angles. The poles are of timber and generally 12cm in diameter and up to 5m in height; many have wire stays. Most have a single step-iron near the top and metal discs with identification numerals. Only one has a timber cross-piece with ceramic insulators near the top. All however have the notches for the cross-piece.

The keeper of the Scatwell estate provided the information that this line of poles had been constructed for a field telephone system from Scatwell over to Cabaan Lodge in Glen Orrin in the 1920s. At this time Glen Orrin was part of the Scatwell Estate which was owned by Sir William Coats Cross (1876-1947), a Glaswegian industrialist. Cabaan Lodge is now submerged under the Orrin Reservoir, the Orrin Dam

Fig. 5: Cabaan Lodge before the Orrin dam © Iain Mackay

being constructed in 1959 as part of the Conon valley hydro-scheme (MacKay 2004). The keeper also reported that the line of poles continues for a further 2km SW from Loch Aradaidh but disappears under the reservoir. Sir William established the telephone system to facilitate communication between Scatwell House and Cabaan Lodge, thus negating the need for the two keepers to climb to suitable vantage points and signal the information that a shooting party was planning to visit Cabaan.

Another local resident, who had been born and brought up in Scatwell, provided the information that her father, as a boy, remembered the telephone line in the 1920s. The telephone was a "wind-up" affair, a hand cranked one possibly similar to Fig. 6: "Rural and other telephones that were not on a common battery exchange had a magneto hand-cranked generator to produce a high-voltage alternating signal to ring the bell of other telephones on the line and to alert the operator" (Wikipedia 2019).

Similar systems to this have been reported on other Highland Estates. Surely the story of this telephone system with its tangible remains is worth recording for posterity. It is a small fragment – a "vignette" – of the stalking scene of previous days.

References

MacKay, I. (2004) *The Last Highland Clearance*. Torgormack: Bidean Books

Wikipedia: The Free Encyclopedia (2019) *Telephone* (online). Available from <https://en.wikipedia.org/wiki/Telephone>

Fig. 6: Wooden wall telephone with hand-cranked magneto generator. Biswarup Ganguly © CC BY 3.0

6: Scotland's Rock Art Project (ScRAP)

Personal Observations on a Selection of Sites Visited and Recorded in 2018

by Alan Thompson

Around 5,000 years ago, people in Scotland carved mysterious symbols on rock surfaces across the landscape. We call these prehistoric carvings 'rock art' and, if we look carefully, we can still see traces of them today. Thousands of prehistoric carvings are known in Scotland, and there may be many more waiting to be discovered. They were clearly important to the people that created them, but we know little about how they were used, or what purpose they served (Scotland's Rock Art Project 2019).

Origins of the Project

Members of NOSAS have been involved in finding and recording prehistoric rock art for more than fifteen years. The main initiative came from John Wombell who led the Ross-shire Rock Art Project (RRAP) which aimed to locate and record all the prehistoric rock art in our area. It was very successful in finding new examples, recording them using GPS, drawings, and photography (Fig. 1), and as a consequence John and others built up a body of practical and local knowledge about the subject.

At about that time photogrammetry was being used experimentally to record rock art in the Northumberland and Durham Rock Art Project (NADRAP) (England's Rock Art 2019). Photogrammetry uses a set of photographs to produce a representation of the 3D surface of the rock, which can be processed to show details which may not otherwise be visible, or in some cases may only be visible under special

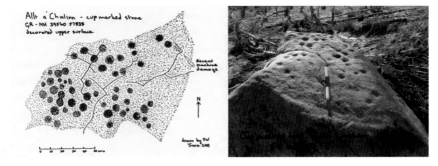

Fig. 1: Drawing and Photograph from RRAP work

lighting conditions. The method was not simple, requiring careful calibration, fixed cameras and expensive specialist software, but some excellent results were obtained, and the potential of the technique was clear.

In 2013 we became aware of free online photogrammetric processing services such as 123D-Catch (now discontinued) and ARC3D (2019). Our first experiment with rock art was in April that year, using a few images taken at Drumtroddan while on holiday in the area and processed using ARC3D (Fig. 2). Although rather basic compared with what we can do today we were pleased with the results and continued to experiment using free online processing services, thus developing a body of knowledge about photogrammetry. In August 2013 Richard Stroud ran a course arranged by Archaeology Scotland demonstrating how to use techniques such as Photosynth (now discontinued) and 123D-Catch to process 3D images and more of the group began to experiment. Subsequently we have adopted Agisoft Metashape (previously Agisoft Photoscan, Agisoft 2019) for all processing.

At that time, we were also considering how to put the RRAP records onto a suitable database for easy access, and extend the project to cover the whole of the Highlands. Getting the records on to the National Monuments Record for the Historic Environment of Scotland (Canmore), and the Highland Historic Environment Record (HER) was not impossible but proved slow and frustrating. Both contain records about rock art. In many cases the records are grouped or within other records and are not easy to search and analyse. Few have

Fig. 2: Drumtroddan. First experiment April 2013

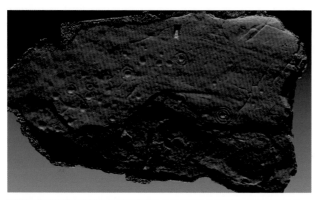

Fig. 3: Easter Backlands of Roseisle 2, processed image from photos by Anne MacInnes

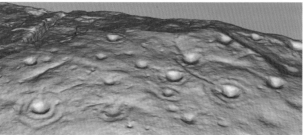

Fig. 4: Perspective view rendered using SketchFab, from the top left of Fig. 3

images available online. Some are based on information from before the advent of GPS and may not have been located in recent times, and others are known but have not yet found their way onto the record.

As part of a review of strategy NOSAS took the decision that it did not want to manage such a project and so when we heard that Dr Tertia Barnett of Edinburgh University was planning a Scotland-wide rock art project, we were immediately keen to take part. The project was to use photography and photogrammetry as a primary recording method and make use of Community groups for field work. Tertia successfully raised funding for the five-year Scotland's Rock Art Project (ScRAP), which began in 2017. NOSAS was an early partner in the project focusing on piloting the field work and data entry. During 2018, as one of a number of Community groups involved with the project, we began serious recording and we now have some good examples to share.

Terminology, and ScRAP Database

We refer to a discrete piece of rock art, including the whole visible rock on which it was carved, as a panel. This is in contrast with everyday English usage which would see a panel as only part of the whole e.g. a panel in a door. The part of the panel on which the motifs have been carved is the carved surface.

Most of the examples below have been recorded on the ScRAP database and will in due course be transferred to Canmore and the Highland HER. Their details, photos and 3D model can be accessed on the ScRAP website (2019) using the panel name or the ScRAP numbers quoted.

Some Examples

When most people hear about 'cup and ring boulders' they think of the famous panels at Kilmartin – wide, flat outcrops of smooth rock onto which cups with multiple concentric rings have been carved. Few panels in our area are like this, but we will start first with one that is – Easter Backlands of Roseisle 2 (Fig. 3). This sandstone panel is both damaged and worn, but the rings around at least 9 and possi-

Fig. 5: Balnafoich 2, photos showing scale of boulder and three cups visible in natural light

Fig. 6: Cups along the edge of the outcrop at Strath Sgitheach

Fig. 7: Dingwall Churchyard. Both sides of Pictish carved stone, with cupmarks

bly 11 cups can be seen. One cup has 3 concentric rings, and three others have two. Looking more closely (Fig. 4), the radial grooves which go out from some of the cups are also visible.

More typically in our area we find one or more simple cups generally on the highest point on rough (medium grained) schist boulders, for example Balnafoich 2 (Fig. 5, ScRAP 3056). Balnafoich 2 is a large boulder of schist, 4.3m by 3.0m by 1.5m high, with three well formed cups at its highest points. The panel is on an east facing slope, near to the confluence of the Rivers Nairn and Farnach (just visible in the background). It is one a group of four panels. A few meters away is Balnafoich 1 (ScRAP 708) which is a flat slab of schist, flush with the ground, having 25 cups on it, and quite different in character to its neighbour.

There are a number of examples of panels which are an outcrop of rock, one side disappearing under the turf and the other a sharp step. The cups are arranged generally along the edge, for example as in Strath Sgitheach, Allt an Criche 2 (Fig. 6, ScRAP 613).

The panels mentioned so far are in their original locations. However, many panels have been re-located, perhaps several times, and re-used for different purposes. A good example is the standing stone in Dingwall Churchyard (Fig. 7, ScRAP 3028). It is recorded in Canmore (12820) as a Pictish Symbol Stone that in 1880 was in use as a lintel over a doorway in St Clement's Parish Church, Dingwall. It has since been moved to the churchyard where it is set upright in a prominent position immediately inside the main gate. It has clearly been broken since the Pictish carvings were made and has cupmarks as well as Pictish carvings on both sides. A few other panels also have carvings on both sides, notably the Heights of Fodderty Stone (ScRAP 2234) and the stone at Brahan House (ScRAP 62).

The panel at Kinmylies in Inverness (Fig. 8, ScRAP 2300) has been built into a field bank. The Highland HER (MHG54253) notes "A cup marked stone, built into a stone dyke at Kinmylies. At least 14 cup marks are visible on the exposed surface" and includes two photographs by an 'unknown photographer'. The photographs give little clue as to the complex motifs on this interesting panel. Alternative processing and a perspective view bring out the full detail (Fig. 9). Note the dumbbell towards the top which also has a faint ring around

Fig. 8: Kinmylies, Inverness. Note the dumbbell with a partial ring around it

Fig. 9: Kinmylies, perspective view rendered using SketchFab

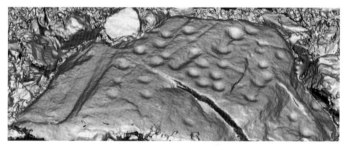

it, in addition to the 29 cups, some of which are joined by grooves, and a 'bar'.

Many of the panels are very worn and we use photogrammetry to pick out details which are so slight that they are often otherwise invisible. In contrast, at Clava there is a panel which retains a crisper appearance. It is one of the kerbstones of the NE Cairn, at its northern edge (Fig. 10, ScRAP 3042). The stone was discovered lying face down in 1931 (Barclay 1990) and has been reset into its current position. The marks made by the tools used to carve out the grooves in the fine sandstone can easily be seen. Note the ring around one of the cups at the far right of this image.

Not all the panels with complex designs are on flat or flattish surfaces. Black Hill 2, a most irregular shaped panel, is covered in cup-marks (Fig. 11, ScRAP 2093). At least one has a surrounding ring, and there are several grooves. The panel is about 70m from Black Hill 1

Fig. 10: Kerbstone of Clava NE Cairn

Fig. 11: Black Hill 2

(ScRAP 1183), a larger flat panel with at least 37 cups, a deeply incised cup and ring, and a dumbbell.

Some personal observations on the panels recorded to date

We don't know the reason why the panels were carved and we can only observe and record the panels which remain today. Many must have been destroyed over the years, many are badly worn, and many have been moved. The remaining sample is small and may be unrepresentative. Despite that, as shown above, no-one can help but be struck by the variety and very different characters of the panels we have seen to date.

Character

On the simpler panels, with just one or a few cups, the cups tend to be at the highest point. Often there is another isolated cup somewhere else on the panel (Rogie 39, Dalreoich 1, Balnafoich 2). Where there are larger numbers of simple cups they are often in an apparently random scatter over a flattish surface, and often of different depths (Cnoc Bhiosta 1, Dalreoich 4). On outcrops, cups are frequently along an edge of the outcrop (various in Strath Sgitheach, and Rogie). Many panels have one larger cup, sometimes with a ring (Balnuarin of Clava, Black Hill 1). The more complex panels have cups, rings, and grooves, and (so far) each has a unique character, some of which have been shown above.

Location

Many of the known panels are in groups, for example Druim Mor, Strath Sgitheach, Rogie farm, Urchany. There is no doubt that they do survive in groups today, and because of that the reply to the perennial question of where to look for new panels is always 'near to known ones'.

Many panels have obviously been moved, but when? There are eight panels built into the cairns at Clava. Some at least must have been carved before being placed in the cairn, and so were 'moved' in antiquity. The history of the stone in Dingwall churchyard has been outlined, from cup-marked stone to Pictish carved stone, broken at some stage, to church lintel and to standing stone. Field clearance must have destroyed many panels, but some remain such as Heights of Fodderty, now rescued and mounted at the Neil Gunn monument. Some are 'in captivity' in museums and gardens. Some have been moved in very recent times, using powerful farm machinery and not always very carefully (Dalreoich 4).

We are told by experts that panels will usually be located on south facing slopes, or in the bottom of river valleys, often overlooking 'good ground', and our sample so far supports that. It is also suggested that they are often near the confluence of rivers (the Balnafoich group is an excellent example), or on route ways, although as yet we don't have enough data for that.

Geology

A major factor in our area is geology. Sandstone forms a ready 'canvas', and some of our more complex panels are on sandstone (e.g. Ardoch). However, most of the panels we have recorded so far are on a grey mica schist, sometimes with garnets. This is medium grained and not at first sight especially promising as a 'canvas'. Some members visited Tiree and recorded the panels there, on Lewisian gneiss, possibly even less promising. And when fossicking (prospecting) we find a lot of boulders of coarse granitic rock with quartz, feldspar and mica crystals of 5mm and larger, and on these we have yet to find any rock art at all.

Conclusions

The attractions of rock art and of the ScRAP project are many, indoor and outdoor, group and individual. The challenge of making sense of the records in Canmore and the local HER; the challenge of finding the panels, known as well as new; fossicking; cleaning and recording on site; examining the 3D models to confirm or amend our field observations; and getting a panel firmly and correctly on the record.

The project is due to run until the end of 2021. We have made a slow start, but at the time of writing recording is well underway. Our impressions will no doubt change as we visit and record more panels. Making sense of the records is challenging and as the number of records increases it will be interesting to see what Tertia Barnett and the other experts ultimately conclude from our work.

Note: Where the images have been uploaded to the ScRAP website they are © HES, all other images are © NOSAS.

References

Agisoft (2019) *Metashape — Photogrammetric Processing of Digital Images and 3D Spatial Data Generation* (online). Available from <http://www.agisoft.com/>

ARC3D (2019) *ARC3D Automatic Reconstruction Cloud* (online). Available from <http://www.arc3d.be/>

Barclay, G. (1991) 'The clearing and partial excavation of the cairns at Balnuaran of Clava, Inverness-shire, by Miss Kathleen Kennedy, 1930-31', *Proceedings of the Society of Antiquaries of Scotland*, 120, pp. 17-32 (online). Available from <http://journals.socantscot.org/index.php/psas/article/view/9377>

England's Rock Art (2019) *The Northumberland and Durham Rock Art Pilot Project* (NADRAP) (online). Available from <http://tinyurl.com/y5j72bh4>

Scotland's Rock Art Project (2019) *Scotland's Rock Art Project* (online). Available from < https://www.rockart.scot>

7: Huts, Cups and Barrows
The Prehistoric Landscape of Buntait, Glenurquhart

by James McComas

The corridor of Glen Urquhart connects Loch Ness and the Great Glen to the east with Strathglass to the west. The scattered upland settlement of Buntait is situated on south facing slopes towards the western end of Glen Urquhart with the well known Clava type chambered cairn at Corrimony less than a mile distant. Despite having no scheduled monuments at the time of writing, Buntait boasts an impressive array of upstanding prehistoric archaeological features. These include hut circles or roundhouses, field systems, burnt mounds and rock art. Not only are the field systems extensive and some of the hut circles very well preserved, but also there are a couple of ditched barrow features. Locally, only Garbeg is comparable in terms of prehistoric remains.

The Glenurqhuart Story by Alistair Mackell published in 1982, provides a useful if perhaps now outdated introduction:

Not far from the Corrimony Burial Cairn, on Buntait lands, was a settlement of some considerable size where clearly marked hut circles and cairns suggest a community practising primitive agriculture and a boundary wall, which can still be traced, may have served to protect domestic animals from prowling wolves or other marauding wild animals. Some of these circles are 30 feet in diameter and in the centre of at least one, is a depression which may have been a fireplace. These circles are low banks of stones covered with grass or heather about 2 feet high and 4 feet wide at the base. It is difficult to imagine one large roof covering such an expanse, but if so, it would probably have been formed of wattles and thatched with heather or turf, giving, when complete, a dome – shaped appearance. In each case there is a break in

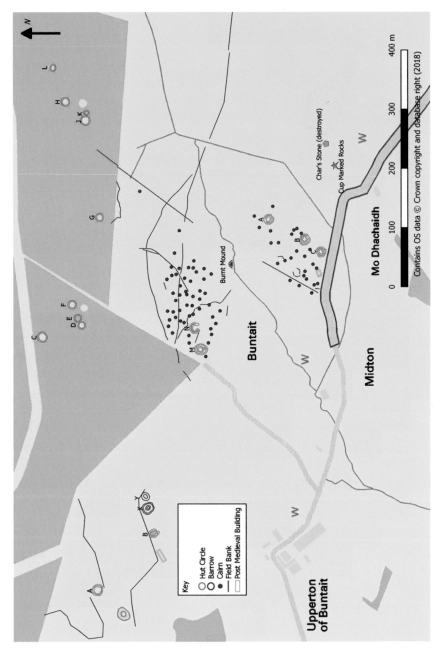

Fig. 1: Detailed map of Buntait showing the principal prehistoric features

Fig. 2: Model of an unfinished hut or roundhouse with clubbed entrance. The construction shown may well be similar to roundhouses at Buntait © Jeremy Fenton

the circle at the south east which indicates the entrance. In other parts of Scotland where these structures have been carefully examined, hearth paving stones have been discovered, but we are unable to reconstruct much of the everyday life of the people of these long bygone days, and we can merely conjecture that they combined hunting with their primitive agriculture, for the Highlands were rich in wildlife.

The main group at Buntait consists of 13 hut circles (Canmore ID 12242) labelled A to N on the map (Fig. 1), with a further three huts (Canmore ID 12243) labelled A to C to the south. These huts are all basically circular with diameters of between 6 and 13 metres and entrances in the SE where they can be identified. Construction appears to consist of rubble, or rubble and turf, walls enclosing a central internal living space. Timber post rings would most likely have supporting a coned thatched roof. Although the term hut circle somewhat belies the fact that these would have been sizeable buildings, it does however allow for the possibility that they were perhaps not all domestic houses.

The huts are associated with prehistoric field systems made up of a network of curved earth banks and areas within, where stone has been cleared for cultivation. Clearance cairn heaps survive presum-

Fig. 4: Aerial image of hut circles M and N with field system © Alan Thompson

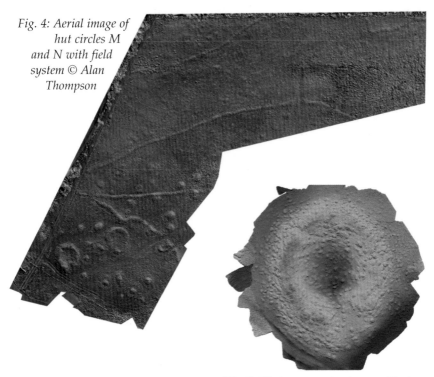

Fig. 3: Photogrammetry image of hut circle 'M' © Alan Thompson

Fig. 5: Hut circle 'G' in the forest at Buntait. NOSAS field trip, January 2017

ably at the edges of these plots and form part of the overall footprint of prehistoric land use surrounding the domestic structure, however the evidence left on the ground today can be difficult to interpret. Similar upland hut circle sites, such as at Achany Glen near Lairg, have been dated to the Bronze Age (McCullagh and Tipping 1998). A settlement in nearby Garbeg, excavated in 2014 by the University of Aberdeen's Northern Picts Project (Noble and Sveinbjarnarson 2016), yielded dates of c.1500 BCE. However, although we might tentatively favour a Bronze Age date for the Buntait huts, it should be noted that roundhouse construction does continue into the Iron Age, and so without radiocarbon dating we can by no means be certain as to the period in which they were built.

One of the best upstanding examples of a roundhouse at Buntait is "M" (Fig. 3), which is 9.5m in diameter and has surviving walls up 0.6m in height. It also features a clubbed or extended entrance in common with several of the other huts. The photogrammetry quadcopter image (Fig. 4) shows the wider landscape with hut circles M and N in the bottom left and field system(s) made up by small cairns and a number of curvilinear dykes. The image extends up to the forest boundaries to the north and west.

Whilst the roundhouses and their associated field systems are at least partially preserved on the rough grazing land, 20th century forestry has broken up the group and 9 of the huts can only be found by venturing deep into the trees. Some of the huts in the forestry have certainly been damaged by forestry ploughing, especially in the western group. However it is perhaps surprising that the tree planting generally respects the hut footprints. Conversation with local former foresters led me to understand that they were local men and knew of the features there, so left the huts unploughed. However subsequent planting has apparently taken place right up to the edges of these sites and the associated field systems have been entirely planted over (Wordsworth 2003).

Two of the huts are in the forest are directly adjacent or contiguous, with one (J) being almost 13m in diameter and the other (K) only 6m. This led to some speculation during a NOSAS field visit on the possible relationship between the two, assuming both were in use simultaneously. Theories varied. Did the larger one serve as an unroofed

Fig. 6: Aerial image of barrows 'X' and 'Y' © Alan Thompson

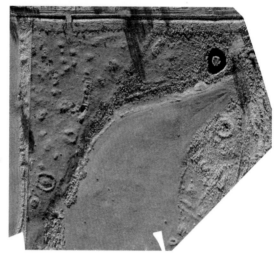

Fig. 7: Aerial image of the barrows at Buntait and the wider landscape processed with photogrammetry © Alan Thompson

Fig. 8: Stood on the larger barrow, looking across to the smaller: Photograph from a field visit which took place for Highland Archaeology Festival, October 2017

byre, whilst the smaller was a roofed domestic living space? Or might they have both been domestic dwellings with the smaller one being perhaps the modern equivalent of a "granny flat"? Current thinking however suggests that Bronze Age farming landscapes were dynamic environments where initial domestic use of a round-house may not have lasted more than a generation. The site could then have served as an animal byre for a period and then in turn as a vegetable plot whilst domestic houses were perhaps established elsewhere in the vicinity. As such, although it is tempting to assume that groups of hut circles were inhabited contemporaneously, this may well not have been the case (Halliday 2007, Romankiewicz and Mann 2017).

The Western most part of the settlement contains two more huts, A and B, plus two other features labelled X and Y which are described on the record as cairns (Canmore ID 12259) (Fig. 6). The whole field, which contains remnants of field systems as well as post medieval settlement, can be clearly seen in the aerial quadcopter image (Fig. 7). Both X and Y have outer ditches and the larger of the two is also surrounded by a 15m diameter surrounding bank. At first glance X almost resembles a hut circle with a large cairn in the middle, albeit one without any obvious entrance.

In discussions with several knowledgeable archaeologists, a number of different interpretations for these features have been proposed. One theory is that they are Pictish burial barrows. However feature X in particular seems to demonstrate distinct differences of both size and form to those found at Whitebridge, Garbeg and elsewhere (McComas 2016). Another suggestion is that they are Bronze Age burial barrows. A few miles to the north of Buntait, at Urchany is a recently scheduled Bronze Age bowl barrow (Highland HER MHG56050). Although larger in scale and featuring a causeway (perhaps a later addition), the Urchany barrow does seem to demonstrate many similarities in form to feature X at Buntait. Y is smaller still, shows signs of disturbance (possibly by the addition of clearance) and lacks the distinctive outer bank of X, but could still also "qualify" as a Bronze Age barrow. As ever, excavation would probably be needed to prove the point.

A Bronze Age date might place these barrows in the same very broad period as the hut circles and field system, and indeed

Corrimony chambered cairn (Canmore ID 12256), which is visible just across the glen. Alastair MacKell in *The Glenurquhart Story* (1982) goes on to posit a possible direct relationship between the Buntait huts with Corrimony cairn; "It can never be proved that the chambered cairn at Corrimony was the burial place of some renowned chief of the Buntait settlement, but it may easily have been so". This may indeed be a considerable stretch, but these possible Bronze Age barrows together with other prehistoric features at Buntait could make a connection more plausible, even if primary use of the sites might be separated by many generations.

On an early NOSAS visit to Buntait, a colleague and I were able to locate a cup marked panel under turf which had eluded RCAHMS on their previous visit. The cup marked rock (Canmore ID 12251) is close to the site of Char's stone (Canmore ID 12257), a standing stone which has sadly been broken within living memory (these features can be found in the SE portion of map Fig. 1). The OS Name book 1876 -1878 reports that Char's stone "applies to a Standing Stone about four feet high three feet broad and two feet thick. There is a tradition in the district that this stone marks the grave of one of the King of Denmark's Sons named Char, nothing further appears to be known about the history of this stone. It is the property of The Chisholm of Erchless Castle". Like Monie's stone at Corrimony (Canmore ID 12255) however, there is little doubt that its origins are much earlier. Clearly the site, which surmounts a gentle knoll with a commanding view of the district, had some significance in prehistory.

On subsequent visits we found that the area around the cup marked rock had been mechanically stripped, and we identified a further panel decorated with a single cup a metre or so away. We also recorded another interesting cup and ring marked rock a few hundred metres to the east (Canmore ID 259329). Examination of the original panel revealed a much worn surface with well over 50 cups, many linked by distinctive troughs (Fig. 9).

Theories about the purpose of cup marked stones may never be resolved, but some of the more persuasive arguments hold that they might function as territorial markers or posts on important route ways. They are generally thought to date from the late Neolithic or early Bronze Age although they are frequently found incorporated

Fig. 9: Cup marked stone at Buntait. To assist with recording the stone for Scotland's Rock Art Project we marked the cups with small lengths of yellow dowelling and connecting troughs with green

into Bronze Age monuments, such as at Corrimony chambered cairn (Bradley 1997). Even if the cup marks and the standing stone do predate the hut circle settlement below them, it seems plausible that they may still have held some significance for the inhabitants.

As will be evident above, my primary focus at Buntait has been on the prehistoric. However, some considerable time was also spent tracking down a much later feature. Upon reading *A Bridge to the Past: An Oral History of the Families of Upper Glenurquhart* (English 2009), I was immediately struck by a photograph of a neatly constructed well, described at being Curadan's Well at Buntait. However the well was then not listed in the archaeological record and it was only finally located with the aid of local knowledge.

The well is named after St. Curadan who lived in the 8th Century AD. William Mackay in *Urquhart and Glenmoriston; Olden Times in a Highland Parish* (1914) states:

Contemporaneous with St Adamnan was Curadan, or Kiritinus, surnamed Boniface, an Irishman who for sixty years preached to the Picts and Scots, and who became bishop and abbot of Rosemarkie, where he died at the age of eighty. To him was dedicated the old chapel at Corrimony Clach Churadain and after him is called Croit Churadain (Curadan's Croft) , and Tobar Churadain (Curadan's Well), both on the adjacent lands of Buntait. The neighbouring churches of Bona and Struy were also dedicated to him. According to tradition, he and Gorman, a saint who gave his name to the hill called

Suidh Ghuirmein, or Gorman's Seat, near Corrimony, were the first to evangelise the people of the Braes of Urquhart. Whether that be true or not, these dedications and place-names show how intimately associated he was with the district.

Of course there is no current evidence to date the well to the early medieval period, or even definitively to say that this is the same well mentioned in the text. However it is a good story and the well (Canmore ID 358418), still fed by fresh water, is certainly worth a look. It makes a diverting further addition to an already fascinating group of archaeological features at Buntait.

Many thanks to the Girvan family for allowing NOSAS access to the area. If you are planning to visit these sites please contact the estate first and respect the Scottish Outdoor Access Code.

References

Bradley, R. (1997) *Rock Art and the Prehistory of Atlantic Europe: Signing the Land.* London: Routledge

English, P.R. (2009) *A Bridge to the Past: An Oral History of Families of Upper Glenurquhart.* Inverness: Speedprint

English Heritage (2011) *Prehistoric Barrows and Burial Mounds* (online). Available from <http://tinyurl.com/y4pbgejw>

Halliday, S P (2007) 'Unenclosed round-houses in Scotland: occupation, abandonment, and the character of settlement'. In *Beyond Stonehenge: Essays on the Bronze Age in Honour of Colin Burgess.* ed. by Burgess, C., Topping, P. and Lynch, F. Oxford: Oxbow Books, 49–56

MacKay, W. (1914) *Urquhart and Glenmoriston; Olden Times in a Highland Parish,* Second Edition (online). Available from <https://archive.org/details/urquhartglenmori00mack>

Mackell, A. (1982) *The Glenurquhart Story.* Inverness: Inverness Field Club

Fig. 10:
Curadan's well

McComas, J. (2016) *The Picts at Garbeg and Whitebridge* (online). Available from <https://nosasblog.wordpress.com/2016/02/18/the-picts-at-garbeg-and-whitebridge/>

McCullagh, R. P. J. and Tipping, R. (ed.) (1998) *The Lairg Project 1988-1996: The Evolution of an Archaeological Landscape in Northern Scotland.* Edinburgh: Scottish Trust for Archaeological Research

Noble, G. and Sveinbjarnarson, O. (2016) 'Garbeg, Drumnadrochit. Excavation', *Discovery and Excavation in Scotland*, New Series, Volume 16, 117. Tisbury: Cathedral Communications

Ordnance Survey, *Name Books 1876-1878, Inverness-shire Mainland volume 56* (online). Available from <http://tinyurl.com/yy6rf9mh>

Romankiewicz, T. and Mann, B. (2017) *Excavating Prehistoric Roundhouses: Guidance on good practice and effective outcome for future research* (online). Available from <http://tinyurl.com/y49hrlyz>

Wordsworth, J. (2003) *Archaeological Survey of Conifer Plantations in Scotland* (online). Available from <http://tinyurl.com/y6bhxlse>

Fig. 1: Inside the Lovat Estate Office

Fig. 2: An office drawer full of maps

Fig. 3: The George Brown book of maps

8: The Lovat Estate Map Project

by Roland Spencer-Jones

In 1756 a young man had been sent by his employers to Coigach, a rough, remote area on the west coast of Scotland, just north of Ullapool. He wrote back to those employers on 21st July:

The estate of Coigach is a very large country, and the subject difficult and tedious to measure, being little else but high mountains with scattered woods, steep rocky places, and a number of lochs in the valleys, which with the great distance there is between houses makes me obliged to sleep in the open fields for several nights together, which is dangerous in a climate where so much rain falls. I wish (you) would condescend to allow me a tent or otherwise I'll have great difficulty to go through. There is no such thing as sleeping in their houses in the summer time, they are so full of vermin (Adams 1979: 10).

The man was Peter May, an Aberdeenshire land surveyor. His employers were the Commissioners for the Board of the Forfeited Annexed Estates. After Culloden the British (London) government forfeited, and therefore took possession of, the estates that had "come out" in the 1745 rebellion. Six years later, in 1752, an Annexing Act was passed. Three years after that, in December 1755, the Board of the Forfeited Annexed Estates finally met for the first time. They wanted to know what lands they now administered, in order to both identify their current value and rental income and to improve the economic performance of those lands. They therefore appointed land surveyors for the main 13 estates that were their responsibility, including the estates of Cromartie (the Mackenzie Estate, and hence Coigach) and Lovat. At that stage Lovat land was centred on the inner Beauly Firth

77

but also included the length of Glen Strathfarrar, Stratherrick and Fort Augustus. Guidelines for the surveying work to be done were drawn up by one of the Board members, Lieutenant-Colonel David Watson, the man who had supervised William Roy in his military survey of 1747-55 (Hewitt 2011: 20). Peter May, a relatively unknown Aberdeenshire surveyor, was appointed to survey the two estates. He subsequently delivered to his employers a series of detailed maps of the entirety of the land he and his team had surveyed.

A definitive book by Ian Adams on Peter May, published in 1979 (Adams 1979), listed many of his Lovat maps as "wanting", i.e. missing. However, some people had gained access to these maps in the Lovat Estate Office in Beauly in previous years, although access had become difficult in recent decades. A determined effort by NOSAS member (and current Chair) Roland Spencer-Jones to see the maps relating to Urchany was eventually successful. That search was driven by the needs of a NOSAS field survey of the Lands of Urchany conducted in April 2015. Having noticed that there were hundreds of maps in the estate office, some of which were not familiar to the estate staff, Roland in early 2017 suggested to the estate manager, Iain Shepherd, that a full cataloguing of the map archive might be helpful for both parties. Over the next six months each of the many drawers and shelves of the map archive were opened and their constituent maps entered on to a spreadsheet, whose columns represented the important categories of: date, title, author or surveyor, dimensions, scale, map format, map condition and finally notes made by the cataloguer. The estate was interested to know which maps had been used in land dispositions, as some were, so this added another column.

The result was a detailed catalogue containing over 400 separate maps and a book of 64 maps (1798-1800) by George Brown, Peter May's nephew. Some of these maps were well known to the estate, whilst some had not been looked at for decades. The list included five Peter May maps out of the eight he was known to have surveyed on the Lovat Estate. The majority of the maps were made in the 19th century, during which two names predominated: John Boulton (maps 1823-1851) and David Gordon (maps 1841-1890). The earliest maps were the Peter May ones. Any earlier estate maps, if they existed, may have been destroyed in the burning of Dounie Castle, the seat of the

*Fig. 4:
NOSAS
members using
the scanner*

Lovats, after Culloden. The maps varied in size, condition, detail and relevance. There had always been an aspiration to digitise the maps, and then upload them to the website of the National Library of Scotland (NLS), as the Dumfries Archival Map Project (McConnell 2019) had done. However, this suddenly became a possibility in early 2018 as the estate considered moving its office. The maps were taking up office space and could instead be deposited in the Highland Archive. However, a digital copy of the maps on the office computers would mean they would still be easily consulted, even if the originals were in Inverness, 13 miles away.

Consequently, a decision was made by the estate to hire an A0 flat-bed Versascan scanner from GenusIT in Warwickshire in order to scan the entire map archive. The labour to do this would be provided by NOSAS members. During a very focussed and energetic week in April 2018 all the maps were processed in what can best be called an industrial production line. A small team of people processed each map, drawer by drawer, shelf by shelf – they had to locate it, unroll it, check it against the list, dust and clean it, then pass it to the scanning team who laid it on the flat-bed, while the scanner operator controlled the scanning process on a computer and gave each map a unique scanning number. The resultant huge TIFF files were then backed up at the end of each day.

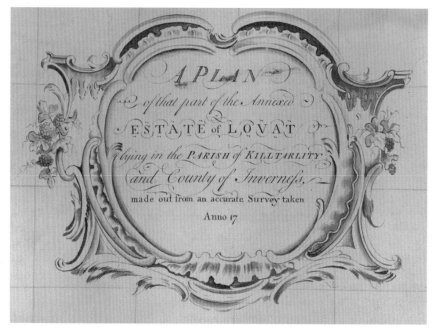

Fig. 5: The artwork from Peter May's Kiltarlity map © Lovat Highland Estates

Fig. 6: An artist's impression of 18th century surveying © Cathy Dagg

At the end of the week, the team had scanned over 400 maps, as well as the 136 pages of a book of maps of the area around Beauly by George Brown. There were in addition 17 old maps from other local estates. This generated more than 200 GB of data, including 900 TIFF images, many of which individually exceeded 500 MB each. Fifty-seven maps were too large to be scanned in one go, even on the 0.8x1.2m flat-bed surface. They were therefore scanned in parts. One huge map (1.4x3.2m) required seven scans. The images were then further processed, which included rotating, cropping, and a JPEG copy made. The NLS then received the maps, stitched together those that were in separate scanned images, and uploaded them to their website: https://maps.nls.uk/estates/. There are now over 400 map images available to look at from anywhere in the world.

What's the importance of these online maps? What do they show? Many of the maps were commissioned to resolve boundary uncertainties or disputes, with adjoining estates. Others relate to intended improvements of the estate property and land. In addition:

● The maps provide snapshots of historical time. Most of the maps are dated, so comparing parts of the estate over time allows change to be observed. For example:

○ Two maps of the arable land of Urchany show the change in agricultural practice, often described as "The Improvements", occurring at the end of the 18th century. In 1757 the Peter May map shows what appear to be collective fields in the runrig system. By the time of the 1800 George Brown map the land has been consolidated into three farms, whose occupiers are identified by name.

○ The rapid growth of Beauly in the early 19th century is shown in a series of maps. The 1757 map shows 21 houses plus the priory ruin. By 1800 there are over 50 houses on the George Brown map, and a small John Boulton map of 1832 shows "The New Town of Beauly" containing 85 dwellings.

● The maps are works of art. The penmanship and calligraphy reflect the skill of the cartographers. Peter May was a leading figure in the "North East School of Scottish Land Surveyors" (Adams 1979: xxv). He learnt and passed on to other developing surveyors the cartographic conventions that included: borders, a scale, a decorated calligraphic title, house style, rig, woodlands, etc. These maps were usu-

Fig. 7: Three maps, three different ways of drawing houses © Lovat Highland Estates

ally started by drawing with lead pencil, which was then overdrawn in various coloured inks or paints. The tools were quills and brushes, rulers and set-squares. There was little margin for mistakes, no rubbing out. The larger maps must represent many days of drawing.

● The maps are the product of considerable surveying skill. The quote by Peter May that starts this article describes the challenges of surveying and measuring the undulating and often mountainous landscape of the Highlands. In the 1750s the simple equipment available to him was a Gunther chain, a cross-post, a plane table, and a circumferometer. The latter was an instrument capable of measuring horizontal angles. It preceded the first simple theodolite, which was not available until Jesse Ramsden developed one in 1787, in Yorkshire. The ways of using surveying equipment in the late 18th century, particularly the simple linked chain, are well described by a Borders surveyor in a book published in 1812, revised in 1849 (Ainslie 1849: 16-41).

● The maps allow a sequencing of cartographic convention, e.g. in the depiction of houses. From the maps in Fig. 7, the development of house symbols over time can be followed. Between 1757 and 1871, house depiction changes, particularly from the 3-D images in 1757 to the plan images in 1798.

In conclusion, the digitisation of the maps allowed those of us who were involved to undertake a fascinating journey into a variety of different worlds – dusty archives, modern scanning techniques, conservation and curation of old maps, the map-makers as individuals and artists, surveying before modern equipment, the distinction between ownership and copyright, etc. And the end result is that a map archive that was trapped in shelves and drawers, difficult to access for modern historians and archaeologists over many years, is now freely available to view on the NLS website from anywhere in the world. Now, that's a success story!

References

Adams, I. (ed.) (1979) *Papers on Peter May, Land Surveyor 1749-1793*. Edinburgh: Scottish History Society

Ainslie, J. (1849) *A Treatise on Land Surveying* 2nd Edition. Edinburgh & London: William Blackwood & Sons

McConnel, A. (2019) *Dumfries Archival Mapping Project* (online). Available from <https://www.facebook.com/Dumfries-Archival-Mapping-Project-571182229681530/>

Hewitt, R. (2011) *Map of a Nation: A Biography of the Ordnance Survey* 2nd Edition. London: Granta Books

9: The Joys and Trials of Documentary Research

by Anne Coombs

In February 2013 a group of NOSAS members went on a walk along the shore of Loch Fleet from Skelbo to Embo. The walk was part of SCAPE Trust's Scotland's Coastal Heritage at Risk Project (SCHARP) to update the condition of known archaeology along the shore. We soon came across the remains of several fishing boats. These had not been recorded during a SCAPE survey some 10 years earlier (SCAPE 2019), as it did not cover Loch Fleet and the Dornoch Firth. The boats are recorded on the Historic Environment Record (MHG29229), but with only a short Northern Times (1995) newspaper report and the accepted story that these boats belonged to the nearby fishing village of Embo and were abandoned on Skelbo shore after the First World War.

SCAPE (Scotland's Coastal Archaeology and the Problem of Erosion) in the form of Jo Hambly and Ellie Graham led a group to survey and record a total of 17 of these boats in detail over a cold weekend in February 2014 (Hambly 2015, SCAPE 2017). Following this it was felt that the story of these boats was sufficiently recent to follow up with documentary research. Initially this seemed a simple project. A day in the archives in Wick, checking the records of boats registered in Wick, provided a long list of named boats with owners, some with addresses. This was hopeful. It was surely now just a matter of going to Embo and speaking to the families to find the descendants of the owners of the boats and hear the story first hand?

In the event, further documentary research was needed before approaching the people in Embo. Armed with the list of boat owners' names, the next obvious place to look was the Highland Archive

Fig. 1: Sternpost of Zulu fishing boat on Skelbo Shore

Fig. 2: Research in Wick Archives © SCAPE

Centre where the local census returns can be viewed. Normally, the census is a wonderful resource providing place of residence, names and relationships enabling a researcher to add colour and depth to an archaeological site. Sadly, in the case of the Embo boat owners, this did not happen. Embo, like so many fishing villages along the Moray Firth, has a number of quirks which makes normal research methods less effective. As a planned village dating from the early 1800s, Embo was originally made up of five rows of houses set at right angles to the shore and which were named in the 1901 census as 1st Back Street, 2nd Back Street, 3rd Back Street, 4th Back Street and Front Street. School Street and Gate Street were added after 1901. Very few of the registered fishermen who owned boats had provided their addresses and these names and addresses did not tally with the information in the census.

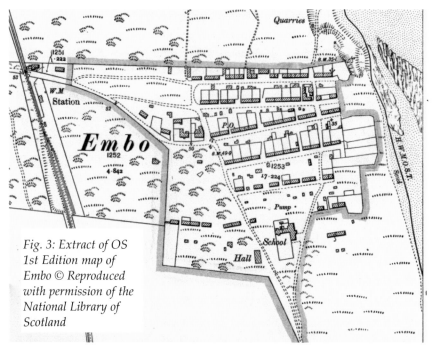

Fig. 3: Extract of OS 1st Edition map of Embo © Reproduced with permission of the National Library of Scotland

Fig. 4: Extract of map by John Thompson 1832 © Reproduced with permission of the National Library of Scotland

In keeping with other fishing villages there are a limited number of surnames; Mackay, Ross, Fraser and Cumming are very common, along with the occasional Grant. In the past, to make life easier, people were given "T" or nick names which would identify, for example, one Mackay family from another. The "T" names were generally not recorded in the census but do appear in some of the boat registrations. The Valuation Rolls, also in the Highland Archive Centre, have the names of the householders, sometimes with "T" names and the address. But again, there was little correlation between boat owner names and addresses.

At this point research foundered – we had lots of names with different addresses and no way of certainly assigning names and families to boats. The most frustrating part was the lack of local memory. Although the people of Embo are rightly very proud of their fishing heritage, the memory of the ownership of the boats has apparently been lost. Families do know that their forefathers were fishermen, but the specifics of who owned which boat has disappeared into the sands of time in much the same way as the boats are disappearing into the sands of Skelbo Bay.

However, research never really ends. There is always another avenue to be followed and it niggled that the date of the original founding of Embo village remained elusive. Maps, of course, were helpful to a certain extent and the invaluable resource of the National Library of Scotland is always fun to trawl through.

When did Embo Fishertown first appear? In 1820 William Skinner records Embo as a place separate from Embo House. In 1832, John Thompson's map shows the Fishertown. The old Statistical Account for Dornoch 1791-99 by Reverend John Bethune refers to "only one boats crew of fishermen, who are neither skilful nor adventurous: they are, therefore wretchedly poor, and of little or no advantage to the place" (Bethune 1793). By the time of the new (second) Statistical Account in 1844 Rev. Angus Kennedy is more positive: "There is indeed a colony of fishermen at Embo; but they only fish for haddocks, small cods, flounders etc. which they sell in the fresh state. The women carry the fish in creels on their backs to this town, and throughout the Parish, and sell it as best they can. Of late years, they have engaged in the herring fishing by hiring themselves to fish cur-

Fig. 5: Street in Embo © Historylinks

ers for the season" (Kennedy 1845).

Local tradition has it that Embo was never a Sutherland Estate clearance village. A tantalising plan dated 1820 with an unreadable signature can be seen in Historylinks Museum in Dornoch showing the proposed fishing village of Embo. The original is thought to be in the National Library of Scotland (NLS). This may be the actual blueprint for the village although there are only 4 rows of cottages and the harbour depicted was never constructed.

All along, in the background to this research into the boats and their owners, was the history of Embo estate. John Malcolm Bulloch states in his book on the Gordon family, *The Gordons of Embo with Others of that Name in the County of Sutherland*, that the Embo estate "was held by the Gordons from the sixteenth century down to 1835, when the second Duke of Sutherland, in his omnivorousness for land, added it by purchase to his colossal holdings" (Bulloch 1907). In some ways the Gordons of Embo are as mysterious as the fishermen. They were very much minor cadets of the Earls of Sutherland with a small estate of two davochs, approximately 832 acres, compared to the millions of acres of Sutherland estates. Robert Home Gordon, son of a Jamaican

Fig. 6: Children watching the lines being baited © Historylinks

plantation owner, inherited the estate in 1804; however the baronetcy went to Sir Orford Home Gordon a cousin who inherited the estate on Robert's death in 1826/7.

It is possible that Robert, who rebuilt Embo House, was also responsible for the establishment of the Fishertown. Certainly in his will of 1812 (NLS, Sutherland Papers) Robert lists "fisheries, boats, fishings and fishtowns" as part of the estate, so it had been estab-lished by then. The abbreviated version of the sasines for Sutherland in Highland Archive Centre lists the changes of ownership of the estate. There were anomalies in the ownership, with a period of four years between 1855 and 1858 when the estate was leased to Davidson & Barkly Company of London, which had extensive landholding in Jamaica and also in Ross-shire. The period may simply have been a way to raise a loan for Sir Orford Gordon, but the estate was sold by his son William on the death of his father in 1858.

It was to clarify this evidence that a visit to the National Library of Scotland was finally undertaken late in 2018 to see the Sutherland Estate Papers held in the Special Collections (313/185 EMBO and ACC 1085/312). The assumption was that the Gordons of Embo

Fig. 7: Street
in Embo
© Historylinks

papers had been lodged in London as this was where the Gordons
lived from the 1850s onwards. However one of the joys of persistent
research is that sometimes there is gold in the dusty documents. It
appears that the sale of Embo estate to the Duke of Sutherland for
£12,000 (NLS, Sutherland Papers) happened not in 1835 as stated in
Bulloch's book on the Gordons of Embo, but in 1858. On the sale of
the estate many of the legal documents relating to Embo estate were
transferred to Sutherland estates and then deposited in NLS. Not only
were the copies of the Gordon family wills placed there, but also
many of the personal documents written on behalf of the inhabitants
of Embo village.

These discoveries have sparked renewed enthusiasm for matching
the fishermen with boats, to wills and rentals. The documents include
details of mothers, fathers, sons and daughters along with "T" names
and rental reference numbers. This will finally allow the story of at
least some of the fishermen and their boats to be filled out and most
importantly given to their descendants. Was Christina's son, Donald
Cummins "Curly", the owner of the boat *Ethel Tweedil*, or was the
owner of the *Ethel Tweedil* a different Donald Cumming married to
Jessie and living at 7 Front Street in 1901? Did Kenneth Mackay, boat
builder, build and own the boat *Commodore* in 1898 or the boat *Love
Spring* in 1901? The final link will be to return to the families in Embo
and present the evidence and see if it makes sense to them before the
documentation is fully compiled and published.

Research is fun but persistence and patience is also required. The accepted sources such as the census and National Archives often provide the answers. However, when they do not it is necessary to go at the problem sideways. Would one have expected so many of the wills belonging to the Gordons of Embo to be in the Sutherland Estate Collection? Surely it would be reasonable to expect them to be in the archives in Kew as the last members of the Gordon family lived in England. There is also the matter of the Jamaican plantations; the slaves who worked on them probably provided Robert Gordon with the money to rebuild Embo House. What happened to them? And as for the scandal caused by Robert Gordon – well that is another story…

References

Bethune, J. (1793) *Statistical Account of Scotland. Part VIII. Number 1. Parish of Dornoch* (online). Available from <https://tinyurl.com/y2g85seo>

Bulloch, J. (1907) *The Gordons of Embo with Other Families of the Name in the County of Sutherland* (online). Available from <https://tinyurl.com/yya2gcae>

Hambly, J. (2015) 'Highland, Loch Fleet. Survey', *Discovery and Excavation in Scotland*, New Series, Volume 15, 102. Tisbury: Cathedral Communications

Kennedy, A. (1845) *Parish of Dornoch* (online). Available from <https://tinyurl.com/yylwddwh>

SCAPE (2017) *SCHARP ShoreDIG: Loch Fleet boat graveyard Data Structure Report* (online). Available from <https://tinyurl.com/y2kqr32h>

SCAPE (2019) *Coastal Zone Assessment Surveys* (online). Available from <http://www.scapetrust.org/html/czas.html>

Northern Times (1995) *Old Embo Wrecks at Fleet's Low Tide* (online). Available from <https://her.highland.gov.uk/monument/ MHG29229>

10: Aerial Photogrammetry and the Future of Plane-tabling

by Meryl Marshall

Over the last three years some NOSAS members have been exploring computer technology and IT as a tool to aid the recording of archaeological sites; elsewhere in this publication we have seen how photogrammetry is being used in the recording of Rock Art. Another development has been that of producing photogrammetric aerial images of larger sites such as townships, castles or forts by using a quadcopter and then processing the images. Most of the developments have been achieved by using programmes which are freely available or at low cost on the internet.

NOSAS has produced many measured plans of sites in the past using a method called "plane-tabling". Plane-tabling is fairly simple

Fig. 1: NOSAS members plane-tabling the Ormond Castle site

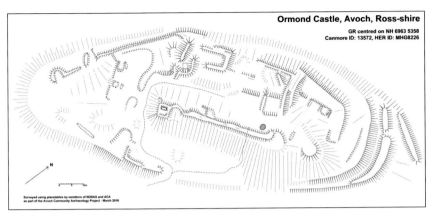

Fig. 2: Completed survey plan of Ormond Castle

and involves drawing a plan by taking measurements through a series of angles from a base station using a metric tape; a kind of triangulation (Royal Commission on the Ancient and Historical Monuments of Scotland 2011). The technique is ideal for a large group of people and can be a sociable activity; we have enjoyed many happy hours in good weather and pleasant surroundings. On a few occasions though, we have encountered the opposite – there are also memories of battling wind and rain and on a couple of occasions even snow. Another advantage is that in plane-tabling a site one becomes very familiar with its subtle nuances. It is proposed here to set out how the two methods of aerial photogrammetry and plane-tabling have been combined in our projects of measured survey over the last three years; considering the pros and cons of each and how they can complement one another.

A plan is much the best way of imparting information on a site and a measured survey is not complete until the results have been drawn up and a plan produced. The plan drawing can be done by hand or by using one of the many drawing programmes available on the Internet, free or purchased. However a plan-drawing has the disadvantage of being 2D in nature. We can overcome this to some extent by using different shadings, descriptions or annotations to indicate height of features, their edges or slopes. Our survey projects have usually included a photographic record and recent advances in photogrammetry have made it realistic for us as amateurs to begin to cre-

Fig. 3: The 3D image produced from the aerial photographs. The full 3D model, which can be rotated, is available on the Sketchfab website

ate and use 3D images.

In Spring 2016 we set out to plane-table survey Ormond Castle (NH 6963 5358, Canmore ID 13572) near Avoch on the Black Isle. The project would also involve taking aerial photographs (APs) using a quadcopter. Our task to complete a measured survey using plane-tables (PTs) was ambitious; not only was the site complex, but it was also big (150m x 65m) and had considerable height discrepancy. Nine PT stations were needed to cover the site. Inevitably the height variations over the site meant that measurements were distorted and the PT positions were not quite correct in their relationship to each other, but this was overcome at the drawing-up stage by using the APs. The PT positions were precisely marked on the ground using spray paint and the photogrammetrically rectified aerial photographs taken from the quadcopter flyover were used to adjust their positions on the plan. The flyover also produced some impressive 3D images of the castle and its features; when viewed using the website Sketchfab they gave a greatly enhanced overall picture of the fortification (Avoch Community Archaeology 2018).

The second plane-tabling project was also a "Castle" site, but a very different one to Ormond Castle. In March 2017 eleven NOSAS members spent a sunny but cold day surveying Kinbeachie Castle (NH

Fig. 4: Plane-tablers in action at the Kinbeachie Castle site

Fig. 5: The gable end of a Laird's House photographed at Kinbeachie Castle in 1959 © Canmore

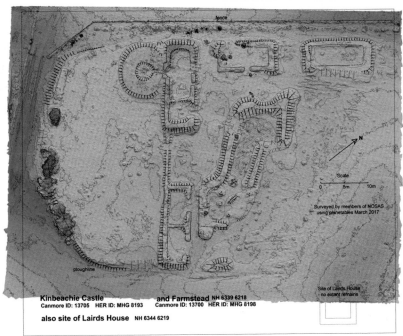

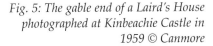

Fig. 6: The plane-table drawing of the Kinbeachie site placed over the photogrammetric image produced from the aerial photographs

6339 6218, Canmore ID 13705) near Culbokie, using five linked plane-tables. The site itself appeared to be that of a farmstead with associated byres and horse gang, there was no obvious evidence of a castle. In addition, and to add to the confusion, the ruins of a "Laird's House" had been photographed in 1959! The day was perfect for a quadcopter "flyover" and a detailed photogrammetric image was produced from the aerial photographs; it fitted perfectly under the plan-drawing produced by the plane-tablers. Could we have drawn the plan from the photogrammetry AP? The possibility began to be considered. And was there a castle at "Kinbeachie Castle"? The APs and plan drawings did indeed show the remains of a tower house, much altered and reused, at the centre of the site. However the "Laird's House", marked as a ruin on the 1st edition OS map, had disappeared completely; it had been on the higher ground to the east of the present site but had been comprehensively ploughed out.

One of the drawbacks of a PT exercise is that it involves a considerable amount of organisation – deciding on a date, seeking permission from the landowner, gathering together the equipment, and sorting out the "teams" for each table. Perhaps it would be quicker and

Fig. 7: Extract from the Roy military map of c. 1750 showing the Old House at Inverlaidnan with its enclosure and associated buildings
© *British Library Board*

Fig. 8: The photogrammetric image produced from the aerial photographs of Inverlaidnan House and surrounds

Fig. 9: The plan drawing of Inverlaidnan House and surrounds for comparison

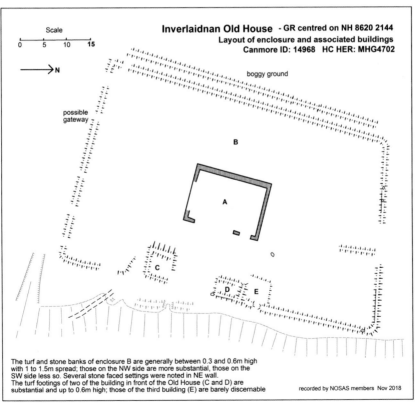

Scale

0   5   10   **15**

→N

Inverlaidnan Old House - GR centred on NH 8620 2144
Layout of enclosure and associated buildings
Canmore ID: 14968   HC HER: MHG4702

boggy ground

possible
gateway

B

A

C

D   E

The turf and stone banks of enclosure B are generally between 0.3 and 0.6m high
with 1 to 1.5m spread; those on the NW side are more substantial, those on the
SW side less so. Several stone faced settings were noted in NE wall.
The turf footings of two of the building in front of the Old House (C and D) are
substantial and up to 0.6m high; those of the third building (E) are barely discernable

recorded by NOSAS members Nov 2018

easier to draw a plan from the photogrammetry image? A third project, in 2018 at Inverlaidnan, provided the opportunity to try this out.

Inverlaidnan is a small estate in the upper reaches of the River Dulnain near Carrbridge with a Laird's House at its centre. This Old House (NH 8620 2144, Canmore ID 14968) had been established in the early 18th century, but by 1851 it was abandoned. The site is a scheduled monument, ID 10481, and of particular interest because it still has the remains of the original enclosure and associated buildings around it; these are marked on the Roy map of c. 1750 (Fig. 6) and the estate plans of 1771 and 1808 (RHP8930 and RHP13916, National Records of Scotland). It had been intended to produce a measured survey of this site and a nearby township as part of the Inverlaidnan and Sluggan project of summer 2018, but by autumn, with winter closing in, we were running out of time. An aerial photogrammetry image of the site had already been produced. This was placed under drawing film on a board and a draft survey drawn up in the field. It needed a second visit to check the details and to determine an accurate scale and orientation. The site was sub-rectangular; it was a simple task to take measurements of the banks in order to secure a scale and to orientate the draft and take a compass bearing for the North arrow.

The second site at Inverlaidnan was an unrecorded township at NH 8582 2161, north of the Old House. It was a very different type of site and presented a different problem. Initially it appeared to be an area of nebulous humps and bumps partly overgrown with juniper bushes. We had the impression that something was there but it was difficult to interpret. The estate plans of 1771 and 1808 were a great help; they showed a township. Once we had this evidence we began to see the fragmentary remains of buildings, a kiln and possible middens. The quadcopter flyover produced a reasonable image, but the features were obscured because of the juniper bushes. It needed two further visits at the drawing up stage of the plan to check and correct the details of the site.

The conclusions are that aerial photogrammetric images can be used to produce a drawing which is just as acceptable as that produced by plane-tabling. It is a much quicker and easier method which involves much less organisation. NOSAS has been fortunate in having members who have the expertise and are able to devote the time and resources to undertaking the flyovers and producing the images. However we would miss the social experience of plane-tabling, of working together towards a common objective. And there are also situations where a quadcopter flyover is not suitable and photogrammetric images cannot be produced – in woodland, for example, or when the weather is doubtful. Consequently both methods can be used in conjunction with one another. The days of plane-tabling are not over just yet.

References

Avoch Community Archaeology (2016) *Ormond Castle, Avoch 3D Model* (online). Available from <https://skfb.ly/VPHJ>

Marshall, M. (2016) *Report of a Survey of Ormond Castle, Avoch* (online). Available from <https://tinyurl.com/y4kbbte8>

Marshall, M. (2017) *Report of a Project to Survey the Site of Kinbeachie Castle, Cullicudden on the Black Isle* (online). Available from <https://tinyurl.com/y65s6umx>

Marshall, M. (2019) *Inverlaidnan and Sluggan/Inchluin, near Carrbridge, Inverness-shire* (online). Available from <https://tinyurl.com/yy2pnplo>

Royal Commission on the Ancient and Historical Monuments of Scotland (2011) *A Practical Guide to Recording Archaeological Sites* (online). Available from <https://tinyurl.com/y3ofluuu>

Other publications available from NOSAS

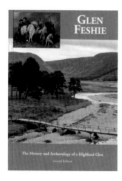

Glen Feshie – the History
and Archaeology of a Highland Glen
by M Marshall, 2nd Edition 2013
978-0-9568786-1-8 – £9

Strathconon – The History
and Archaeology of a NE Highland Glen
by M Marshall, 2011
978-0-9568786-0-1 – £9

Prehistoric Roundhouses
of Wester Ross and parts of Skye
by Anna Welti, Martin Wildgoose
and Jeremy Fenton, 2015 – £5

Available in Highland bookshops or through www.nosas.co.uk